Kids' Guide
to the
ENGLISH LANGUAGE

Books by Marvin Terban

SCHOLASTIC

Building Your Vocabulary

Checking Your Grammar: And Getting It Right

Dictionary of Idioms

Dictionary of Spelling

Punctuation Power: Punctuation and How to Use It

Verbs, Verbs, Verbs: The Trickiest Action-Packed Words in English

Writer's Desk Reference

CLARION/HOUGHTON MIFFLIN

The Dove Dove: Funny Homograph Riddles

Eight Ate: A Feast of Homonym Riddles

Funny You Should Ask: How to Make Up Jokes and Riddles with Wordplay

Guppies in Tuxedos: Funny Eponyms

In a Pickle: And Other Funny Idioms

It Figures! Fun Figures of Speech

I Think I Thought: And Other Tricky Verbs

Hey, Hay! A Wagonful of Funny Homonym Riddles

Superdupers: Really Funny Real Words

Mad as a Wet Hen! And Other Funny Idioms

Punching the Clock: Funny Action Idioms

Too Hot to Hoot: Funny Palindrome Riddles

Your Foot's On My Feet! And Other Tricky Nouns

BOYDS MILLS PRESS

Time to Rhyme: A Rhyming Dictionary

Kids' Guide
TO THE ENGLISH LANGUAGE

by
Marvin Terban

Illustrated by Joe Bartos

CHILDREN'S BOOK-OF-THE-MONTH CLUB
NEW YORK

To my son David, whose command
of the English language is so great,
he could have written this book himself

Kids' Guide to the English Language is a publication of
Children's Book-of-the-Month Club,
1271 Avenue of the Americas, New York, NY 10020

Book design by Joe Bartos

Printed in the United States of America

CONTENTS

INTRODUCTION

There are over 2,500 languages in the world today, and English is one of the three most popular. Some experts estimate that almost a billion people use English as their first or second language.

Wherever you go in the world, you will speak, hear, read, and write English. It's hard to get lost on the subways of Tokyo, Japan, because the signs are in English and Japanese. You can buy an English-language newspaper in every major city of the world. When a plane from

> Mandarin Chinese and Spanish are the other most-used languages in the world.

Asia lands in South America, the pilot and the air traffic controller speak to each other in English. Scientists, politicians, educators, and business people from many different countries speak to each other exclusively in English. The number of people who are learning English in China today is about the same as the number of people who now live in the whole United States!

It's very important for you to use the best English you can. When you write a paper in school, meet new people, apply to college, or try to get a job, you will want to get your ideas across in the best possible way— with no embarrassing mistakes.

But English is very tricky. There are more words in English than in most other major languages. Spelling can be a real challenge. You have to capitalize the right words. Correct punctuation sometimes baffles even college professors. Many words mean

9

the same thing or sound the same way even if they're spelled differently. And some expressions, like "Don't let the cat out of the bag" and "Wet behind the ears" mean something very different from what they seem to mean.

Don't worry. This book will help you. Just look at the Table of Contents that begins on page 5 or in the Index that begins on page 113 to find any topic you need. You're on your way to understanding and using English better.

Chapter 1
The Parts of Speech

To build a house you need building materials like wood, metal, and glass. To build a language you need building materials, too. They're called the **Parts of Speech,** and there are eight of them:

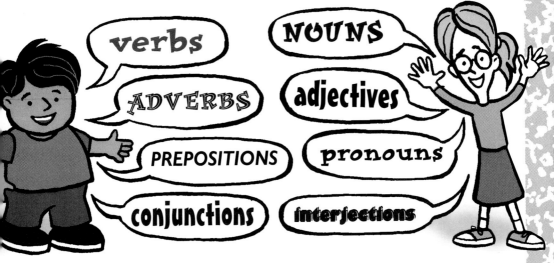

There are over 600,000 words in the English language, and every single word fits into at least one of these eight categories.

VERBS

A **verb** is a word that shows action, being, or doing.

The verb to be
The verb *to be* shows being, not doing: *am, are, is, was, were, be, being, been.*

Verbs can show dynamic action like *running, jumping,* and *bouncing* or quiet action like *thinking, reading,* and *looking.*

Tenses

Tense means the time at which the action, being, or doing happens. There are six main tenses.

The **present** tense expresses an action that is happening right now.

> She **sees** the tap-dancing octopus.

The **past** tense expresses an action that has already happened.

> She **saw** the baby flying the hot air balloon.

The **future** tense expresses an action that is going to happen.

> She **will see** amazing sights on her trip to Mars.

The **present perfect** tense expresses an action that was started in the past and has just finished or is still continuing.

> She **has seen** what she wanted to see, and now she wants to go home.

The **past perfect** tense expresses an action in the past that was completed before another action in the past.

> She **had seen** everything in the museum before it closed.

The **future perfect** tense expresses an action that will be begun and completed in the future.

> She **will have seen** the "Happy Birthday" sign before we shout "Happy Birthday," and the surprise will be ruined.

Helping Verbs

There are twenty-three common helping verbs (sometimes called auxiliary verbs). They're easy to remember if you think of them like this.

3 D's: **do, does, did**

3 H's: **have, has, had**

3 M's: **may, must, might**

3 B's: **be, being, been**

3 —ould's: **should, could, would**

2 —ll's: **shall, will**

The verb *to be*: **am, are, is, was, were**

and **can**

A full verb phrase can have one, two, three, or four words: one main verb and up to three helping verbs.

You **go**.

You *have gone*.

You *will have gone*.

You *should have been going*.

Regular and Irregular Verbs

Most verbs in English are regular. To form their past tenses, they just add **–ed** or **–d**.

Today it walks. Last week it walk**ed**. It has always walk**ed**.

Today it dances. Last week it danc**ed**. It has always danc**ed**.

Irregular verbs, on the other hand, form their past tenses in unusual ways. That's why they're called "irregular." Here are some examples.

Today I... (Present)	Last week I... (Past)	I have always... (Past Participle)
begin	began	begun
bite	bit	bitten or bit
blow	blew	blown
break	broke	broken
bring	brought	brought
buy	bought	bought
catch	caught	caught

Today I... (Present)	Last week I... (Past)	I have always... (Past Participle)
choose	chose	chosen
come	came	come
dive	dove or dived	dived
do	did	done
drink	drank	drunk
drive	drove	driven
eat	ate	eaten
fall	fell	fallen
fight	fought	fought
flee	fled	fled
fling	flung	flung
fly	flew	flown
forget	forgot	forgotten or forgot
freeze	froze	frozen
get	got	gotten or got
give	gave	given
go	went	gone
grow	grew	grown
hang (a picture)	hung	hung
hang (a person)	hanged	hanged
hide	hid	hidden
hold	held	held
keep	kept	kept
know	knew	known
lay	laid	laid
leave	left	left
lie	lay	lain
lose	lost	lost
meet	met	met
ride	rode	ridden
ring	rang	rung
rise	rose	risen
run	ran	run
see	saw	seen
sit	sat	sat
shake	shook	shaken

It might fall.

He looks.

She tripped!

Today I... (Present)	Last week I... (Past)	I have always... (Past Participle)
shine	shone	shone
shoot	shot	shot
shrink	shrunk or shrank	shrunk or shrunken
sing	sang	sung
sit	sat	sat
slay	slew	slain
slide	slid	slid
speak	spoke	spoken
spring	sprang or sprung	sprung
stand	stood	stood
steal	stole	stolen
sting	stung	stung
strike	struck	struck or stricken
swear	swore	sworn
swim	swam	swum
swing	swung	swung
take	took	taken
teach	taught	taught
tear	tore	torn
tell	told	told
think	thought	thought
throw	threw	thrown
wake	woke or waked	waked or woken
wear	wore	worn
write	wrote	written

NOUNS

A **noun** is a word that names a person, place, thing, or idea.

There are more nouns in English than any other kind of word because there are so many people, places, things, and ideas in the world to name.

In the short paragraph below, there are twenty nouns.

> **Consuela**, a **girl** in my **class**, lived in the **country** of **Brookliana** until she was three **years** old. Then she and her **family** traveled with great **courage** by **horse**, **bus**, **boat**, and **plane**, over **mountains**, **jungles**, and **oceans**, to get to **Boston**. Their **house** is on **Renae Road**, near the **mall** that sells those tap-dancing **piglets**.

Articles

The, *a*, and *an* are called *articles*. They are also called "noun signals" because they signal you that a noun is coming up in the sentence. The noun could be the next word, or it could come a few words later, but if you see *the*, *a*, or *an* in a sentence, you can be sure you're going to find a noun soon.

      noun   noun
The dog buried *a* bone.

          noun   noun
The huge, brown, furry dog buried *a* huge, brown, furry bone.

Kinds of Nouns

A noun can be:

Sometimes two or more words together make one proper noun:

Empire State Building
Okefenokee Swamp
Sea of Japan
Lake Titicaca
Central Park West

Common–the name of any person, place, thing, or idea

> *boy, city, toothpick, liberty*

Proper–the name of a specific person, place, or thing

> *Peter, Chicago, Rocky Mountains*

When a noun is proper, it's always capitalized. See *Capitalization* on page 63.

Concrete–a person, place, or thing that you can perceive with any of your five senses—sight, hearing, smell, touch, or taste:

gorilla, pizza, tulip, raindrops, mud, computer

Abstract–a feeling, emotion, passion, idea, or quality:

sadness, freedom, nosiness, honesty, intelligence, patience

Some abstract nouns can be proper, especially in poetry or poetic writing:

The passions that burn in you and me
Are Love and Life and Liberty!

Compound–two or more words used together as one noun:

earthquake, jellyfish, football, rush hour, door knob, fairy tale, battle-axe, sister-in-law, drive-in

Collective–a group of persons, places, or things:

staff, faculty, bouquet, audience, team, flock, assembly, bundle, nation

Did you notice that compound nouns can be written as one word, two separate words, or two words connected with a hyphen? Most compound nouns are single words without hyphens, but if you're not sure, check your dictionary or spell check. See *Hyphens* on page 87.

Even though collective nouns include many people, animals, or things, they are still singular nouns, not plural, because everyone or everything in the group is acting together as one.

The orchestra *is* (not *are*) performing at 8 o'clock.

Uses of Nouns

A noun is the busiest part of speech. Nouns can be used in all of the following nine ways.

Subject

The subject is the word that names the person, place, thing, or idea that the sentence is about. Every sentence must have a subject. Without a subject, there's no sentence. The subject always performs the action of the verb.

So, to find the subject, first find the verb and ask yourself, "Who or what is doing this?" The answer will be the subject.

> An elephant the size of Toledo nimbly walked across the tightrope while juggling three watermelons.

What's the verb? *Walked.* Who walked? An *elephant.* So *elephant* is the subject of the sentence. The sentence is about the *elephant.*

Complete subjects and simple subjects

In the sentence above about the elephant, *elephant* is the subject. Since it's only one word, we call it the *simple subject.* The six words *an elephant the size of Toledo* are called the *complete subject.* The complete subject is the simple subject and all its modifiers (the adjectives, adverbs, prepositional phrases, etc., that go with it). See pages 22, 23, and 25 to learn more.

> Sometimes the simple subject is also the complete subject:
>
> I tripped over my shoelace and fell right into the barrel of spaghetti sauce.
>
> *I* is the simple subject and the complete subject all in one word.

A simple subject can sometimes be more than one word when the words go together to name one person, place, or thing:

> The Golden Gate Bridge in San Francisco Bay was opened in 1937 and for over 25 years was the longest suspension bridge in the world.

In the sentence above, *The Golden Gate Bridge* is the simple subject because all those words name just one bridge. *The Golden Gate Bridge in San Francisco Bay* is the complete subject.

Direct Object

The direct object is the noun that receives the action of the verb. While every sentence has to have a subject, not every sentence has a direct object, but many sentences do.

To find the direct object, first find the verb. Then ask yourself, "Who or what is the action being done to? Who or what is receiving the action of the verb?" That's the direct object.

> The captain of the hippo football team kicked the coconut over the palm trees.

What's the verb? *Kicked.* Who or what got kicked? The *coconut.* So, *coconut* is the direct object. It didn't do anything. Something was done to it.

Object of a Preposition

A prepositional phrase is a group of words that starts with a preposition and ends with a noun (or pronoun) called the "object of the preposition." The object of the preposition completes the meaning of the preposition. If you write, "She threw the ball to . . ." and just left the sentence like that, it wouldn't be complete. If you write, "She threw the ball to her dog," the word "dog" completes the meaning of the preposition "to." "Dog" is the object of the preposition "to."

In the following sentences, the prepositional phrases are in *italics* (letters that slant to the right), and the objects of the prepositions are in **boldface**.

*While I was snorkeling, I saw fantastic fish under the **water**.*

*Inside his **pockets*** were treasures too amazing to believe.

See *Prepositions* on page 24.

Predicate Noun

The predicate noun always comes after the verb *to be* (see page 11) and always means the same thing as the subject of the sentence.

Mad Murgatroy is the king of this country and can have you kicked out if he wants to!

What's the verb? *Is.* Who is? *Mad Murgatroy.* That's the subject. What is he? *King. King* is the predicate noun. Mad Murgatroy and king are the same person. Mad Murgatroy is the king and the king is Mad Murgatroy.

Sometimes a **predicate noun** is called a **predicate nominative.**

Noun of Direct Address

When you are speaking or writing directly to a person, you sometimes call him or her by name or title. The noun that indicates that name or title is the noun of direct address. The noun of direct address can be a common noun or a proper noun.

I must ask you, *Mrs. Schlepkis*, to stop chewing on the leaves of my Venus's-flytrap plant.

Kid, will you help me carry this grand piano up the stairs to the twelfth floor?

Who is being spoken to in these sentences? *Mrs. Schlepkis* and *kid*. Those nouns are the nouns of direct address because they name the people who are being addressed (spoken to) directly.

See *Punctuating Nouns of Direct Address* on page 82.

Indirect Object of the Verb

The indirect object names the person, place, thing, or idea that receives the action of the verb indirectly.

The monkey sold the rhino his favorite banana.

What's the verb? *Sold*. What got sold? A *banana*. *Banana* is the direct object. To whom did the banana get sold? The *rhino*. That's the indirect object because it's receiving the action of the verb *sold* indirectly.

The monkey baked the rhino a banana cream pie.

What's the verb? *Baked*. What got baked? A *banana cream pie*. That's the direct object. For whom was it baked? The *rhino*. That's the indirect object.

Here's a tip for finding the indirect object. You can sometimes imagine that the words *to* or *for* are in front of the indirect object. *To* and *for* aren't really there, but the sentence won't sound too bad if you imagine one of these words in front of the indirect object.

> The indirect object always comes before the direct object.

        to
The monkey sold ∧ the rhino his favorite banana.

        for
The monkey baked ∧ the rhino a banana cream pie.

These verbs regularly have indirect objects after them: *give, throw, send, show,* and *buy.*

Appositive

An appositive is a noun or phrase that

1. comes after another noun

2. gives information about it

Hyman, *the world's tallest person*, cleans the windows in his apartment without a ladder, and he lives on the ninth floor!

The world's tallest person comes after Hyman and gives information about him. *Hyman* and *the world's tallest person* are said to be "in apposition" with each other.

See *Punctuating Appositives* on page 82.

Possessive Noun

Possession means ownership. A possessive noun names the person, place, or thing that owns something or has a very close relationship with someone.

George Washington's wooden teeth were on display at the exhibit.

George Washington's wife was named Martha.

All possessive nouns must have apostrophes. See *Apostrophes* on page 73.

Object Complement

Sometimes a direct object is not enough by itself and needs another word to finish the meaning of the sentence. An object complement is the word that completes the object.

Last year they elected my uncle *Chief Zookeeper*.

What's the verb? *Elected.* Who got elected? My *uncle.* That's the direct object. What did he get elected? *Chief Zookeeper.* That's the object complement. Without those words, we wouldn't know what job my uncle was elected to.

A fun way to remember the nine uses of nouns is to remember DIP A SPOON:

Direct Object

Indirect Object

Predicate Noun

Appositive

Subject

Possessive Noun

Object of the Preposition

Object Complement

Noun of Direct Address

The lady next door calls her pet skunk *Perfume*.

What's the direct object? *Pet skunk*. What is it called? *Perfume*. That's the object complement because without it we wouldn't know what the neighbor calls her skunk. It completes the direct object.

ADJECTIVES

An **adjective** is a word that describes (or modifies) a noun or a pronoun.

"Modify" means to qualify or limit the meaning of something. If you say "lizard," you could mean any lizard in the world, but if you say "old, wrinkly lizard," you are limiting—or modifying—your meaning to just lizards that are old and wrinkly. You are not talking about any lizards that are young or smooth.

Bright lamp

Fuzzy teddy bear

Wild hat

Rubber boots

An adjective usually answers one of three questions about the noun it is describing:

1 What kind of? "a *yellow* cat" What kind of cat? *Yellow*.

2. How many? "*sixteen* jellybeans" How many? *Sixteen*.

3. Which one or which ones? "*those* dinosaur bones" Which ones? *Those*.

SALE

Laughin boy

An adjective can come right in front of the noun it modifies:

America is a *free* country, and many *brave* people live here.

An adjective can come after a linking verb (like the verb *to be*):

America is *free*, and her people are *brave*.

An adjective can even stand alone without the noun it is describing being in the sentence.

America is the land of the *free* and the home of the *brave*.

In the example above, you can assume that the sentence means that America is the land of free people and brave people, even though the word "people" isn't in the sentence.

Common and Proper Adjectives

Just as nouns can be common and proper (see *Nouns* on page 16), so can adjectives.

A common adjective is just a regular adjective like *happy, huge, sloppy,* and *wonderful.* A proper adjective comes from a proper noun and is always capitalized.

PROPER NOUNS	PROPER ADJECTIVES
Japan	Japanese
Venice	Venetian
Florida	Floridian
Queen Victoria	Victorian
Finland	Finnish
France	French
Shakespeare	Shakespearean

ADVERBS

An **adverb** is a word that modifies a verb, an adjective, or another adverb.

Adverbs answer these questions:

"Where?"
(The hen laid the egg *there*.)

"When?"
(It happened *yesterday*.)

"How?"
(She cackled *loudly* when the egg came out.)

"To what extent?"
(She was *extremely* proud.)

Sitting here

Shouting noisily

Running quickly

An adverb modifying a verb:
>   **Verb**
> He played the tuba *loudly*.

An adverb modifying an adverb:
>   **Adv.**
> He played the tuba *unbelievably* loudly.

An adverb modifying an adjective:
>   **Adj**.
> His tuba playing was *amazingly* loud.

> You can always remember what adverbs modify if you think of the name AVA (**A**dverbs, **V**erbs, **A**djectives).

PREPOSITIONS

A **preposition** is a word that shows how one word in a sentence relates to another.

A preposition often shows location, direction, time, or a relationship between words.

Location: My little brother is hiding *under* the dirty laundry. (Where is he located? *Under* the laundry.)

Direction: My little brother is falling *into* the vat of chocolate syrup. (Where is he going? *Into* the syrup.)

Time: *After* lunch, I have to give my little brother a bath. (When do I give him the bath? *After* lunch.)

At dinner

Relationship between words: My little brother always wants to go *with* me wherever I go. (What is the relationship between my brother and me? He wants to be *with* me.)

There are thousands and thousands of nouns and verbs in English, but only about fifty prepositions. Here are some of the most common.

about	at	down	of	to
above	before	during	off	toward
across	behind	for	on	under
after	below	from	out	until
against	beside	in	over	up
along	between	into	past	upon
among	beyond	like	round	with
around	by	near	through	without

Out of the water

Aboard the boat

With wings

Compound Prepositions

Sometimes two or more words together do the job of a preposition. They are called compound prepositions.

He went to Jupiter *by way of* Pluto.

Romeo waited *in front of* Juliet's balcony for her to come out.

Everyone failed the test *with the exception of* those who passed.

Prepositional Phrases

Every preposition begins a prepositional phrase. ("Phrase" means a group of words.) The first word in a prepositional phrase is the preposition. The last word is called "the object of the preposition."

The shortest prepositional phrase possible is two words long:

The hamster ran *into it*.

But prepositional phrases can be much longer:

prep.   **object of prep.**

The hamster ran *into its magnificent, sound-proof, air-conditioned, state-of-the-art, fully automated cage.*

Preposition or Adverb?

Sometimes the same word can be a preposition in one sentence and an adverb in the next. How can you tell? Easy. If there's an object of the preposition after the word, it's a preposition. If there's no object, it's an adverb.

She ran *out*. (There's no object, so "out" is an adverb modifying the verb "ran" and answering the question "where?")

She ran *out the door*. ("Door" is the object of the preposition "out.")

25

PRONOUNS

A **pronoun** is a word that takes the place of a noun. A pronoun can be used almost every way a noun can be used.

See *Uses of Nouns* on page 17.

If you didn't have pronouns, you would have to keep repeating the noun all the time like this:

> When Jennifer woke up that day, Jennifer realized that that day was Jennifer's birthday. "Jennifer is a teenager at last!" Jennifer cried. "Jennifer has waited thirteen long years to be a teenager. Jennifer deserves something special today, a birthday gift." Jennifer looked into Jennifer's mirror and saw Jennifer. "Jennifer wonders what Jennifer will give Jennifer on Jennifer's special day," Jennifer said to Jennifer in the mirror.

Subject Personal Pronouns
(Used for subjects)

I, you, he, she, it, we, they

Object Personal Pronouns
(Used for direct objects, indirect objects, and objects of prepositions)

me, you, him, her, it, us, them

Possessive Personal Pronouns
(Used to show ownership)

my, mine, your, yours, his, her, hers, its, our, ours, their, theirs

It sounds so much better, and definitely not so weird, when you replace some of the nouns with pronouns.

> When Jennifer woke up that day **she** realized that **it** was **her** birthday. "**I** am a teenager at last!" **she** cried. "**I** have waited thirteen long years to be a teenager. **I** deserve something special today, a birthday gift." **She** looked into **her** mirror and saw **herself**. "**I** wonder what **I** will give **you** on **your** special day," **she** said to **herself** in the mirror.

He plays games.

She talks to them.

Our computer has crashed!

Besides the personal pronouns listed above, there are many other pronouns that take the place of nouns in sentences. Here are some examples.

anybody, both, each, everybody, itself, many, neither, nobody, nothing, several, some, something, that, themselves, what, which, who, whom, and whose.

CONJUNCTIONS

A **conjunction** is a word that joins together words or parts of sentences.

Joining words together:

I'd like five peanut butter *and* jelly sandwiches to go, please.

Joining parts of sentences together:

I ran as fast as I could, *but* the ice cream melted before I got it home.

There are dozens of conjunctions. Here are some that you use every day:

although	when
because	where
if	however
since	therefore
though	whenever
unless	while

Sometimes conjunctions are used in pairs. They're called **correlative conjunctions.**

either/or	both/and
neither/nor	whether/or
not only/but also	just as/so

Wet but happy

Boy and girl

Cookies or ice cream

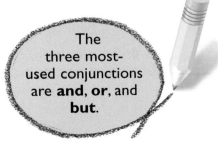

The three most-used conjunctions are **and**, **or**, and **but**.

INTERJECTIONS

An **interjection** is a word that shows strong feelings or emotions.

It is usually a short word that comes at the beginning of a sentence.

Yoo-hoo!

Aha!

Uh-oh.

An interjection can be followed by a comma or an exclamation point. If the interjection shows a really strong emotion, use an exclamation point. See *Exclamation Points* on page 86.

Oh**,** that tarantula is adorable.

Oh**!** You've ruined my favorite pickle costume.

HOW THE PARTS OF SPEECH CHANGE

Sometimes the same word can change its part of speech from one sentence to another. It all depends on how it's used.

       adj.
The **down** elevator is not running, so we have to walk.
("Down" is describing the elevator.)

       noun
I sleep best when the pillow is filled with **down**.
("Down" means "feathers." Feathers are things.)

       adv.
The brontosaurus fell **down** and made the building rumble.
("Down" modifies the verb "fell" and answers the question "Where did the brontosaurus fall?")

       verb
Did she **down** her opponent with just one swipe of her tail?
("Down" is a word that shows action: knocking someone to the ground.)

       prep.
The sprightly squirrel ran **down** the tree.

("Down" is the first word in a prepositional phrase, "down the tree," which shows direction.)

Chapter 2
Sentences and Paragraphs

SENTENCES

What Is a Sentence?

A **sentence:**

- is a group of words
- begins with a capital letter
- contains a complete subject and a complete predicate
- ends with one of three punctuation marks (**.** **?** or **!**)
- makes complete sense

Four Kinds of Sentences

There are four different kinds of sentences in the little dialogue below: **declarative**, **interrogative**, **exclamatory**, and **imperative**. Every sentence in every book, newspaper, magazine, or story that you have ever read fits into one of these four categories.

"You have a banana in your ear."

"What did you say?"

"You have a banana in your ear!"

"Please speak louder. I have a banana in my ear."

Declarative Sentence

"You have a banana in your ear."

This kind of sentence declares a fact, makes a statement, or gives information. It always ends with a **period**.

29

Interrogative Sentence

"What did you say?"

This kind of sentence asks a question. ("To interrogate" means to question.) It always ends with a **question mark**.

Exclamatory Sentence

"You have a banana in your ear!"

This kind of sentence exclaims or cries out with strong emotions or feelings (like anger, frustration, happiness, disgust, surprise, shock, or horror). It always ends with an **exclamation point** (also called an exclamation mark).

Imperative Sentence

"Please speak louder."

This kind of sentence makes a request, asks a favor, or gives a command. It ends with a **period** if it expresses a polite request or gives a mild order like "Open your books." If it expresses strong emotion, it ends with an **exclamation point** like this: "Give me back my chocolate-covered grasshopper this instant!"

Some sentences sound like questions, but they're really imperative sentences. They end with periods, not questions marks.

"Will you kindly take that lamp shade off your head."

"Can you just answer my question without whistling."

"You (Understood)" The subject of every imperative sentence is "you." Because the reader or listener sometimes has to understand that "you" is the subject, it's called "you (understood)."

Imagine four friends talking, and try to identify the four kinds of sentences in the dialogue below.

"There's a test today."
(That's a statement of fact.)

"What's on it?"
(Obviously a question.)

"I forgot to study!"
(Somebody's panicking.)

"Lend me your notes."
(This person needs a favor.)

If you said **declarative**, **interrogative**, **exclamatory**, and **imperative** in that order, you were right!

30

Subjects and Predicates—
The Two Main Parts of Every Sentence

Every sentence can be divided into two parts: the **complete subject** and the **complete predicate**. Everything in a sentence that is not the complete subject is the complete predicate. Everything in a sentence that is not the complete predicate is the complete subject.

What is the **complete subject**? The subject is the person, place, thing, or idea that the sentence is about. It performs the action of the verb. The **complete subject** is usually a noun or pronoun and all the words that go with it.

How do you find the complete subject? First find the verb (the word that shows action or being). Then ask yourself "Who or what is doing this? Who or what is the sentence about?" The answer will be the complete subject. Everything else in the sentence will be the complete predicate.

See *Verbs* on page 11 and *Subject* on page 17.

complete subject
Mrs. Freedman from Joyce Road

complete predicate
has two children, four grandchildren, and one husband.

Complete subjects and complete predicates can be many words long or just one word.

complete subject
The Universal Museum of Old-Fashioned Inventions
on the corner of Shurtleff and Shawmut Streets

**complete
predicate**
closed.

**complete
subject**
She

complete predicate
put of bowl a cherries, bananas, and strawberries on her head and started dancing the fandango to everyone's delight.

The verb is always in the complete predi-cate. Some people call the verb the **simple predicate**.

The **simple subject** is usually one or two main words inside the complete subject, without all the adjectives, adverbs, phrases, and other words that go with it. In the sentence below, the complete subject is nine words long, but the simple subject is only one word long.

complete subject

The tall, scowling history **teacher** on the third floor gives a lot of homework.

simple subject

Sometimes the **complete subject** is so short, it is also the **simple subject**.

> **Roslyn** used to work for the telephone company before she retired to raise tulips.

A complete sentence can be as short as two words:

> "She laughed."

"She" is the complete subject. "Laughed" is the complete predicate.

A complete sentence can actually be as short as one word if that one word is an imperative verb. "Stop!" is a complete imperative sentence. "Stop" is the complete predicate and "you (understood)" is the complete subject, even though it's not expressed. See *Imperative Sentences* and *"You (Understood)"* on page 30.

Word Order

In most sentences, the complete subject comes before the complete predicate.

> Three wild men in gorilla costumes charged out of the mouth of the dark cave.

But sometimes, for variety, the predicate can come first.

> Out of the mouth of the dark cave charged three wild men in gorilla costumes.

Sometimes the complete subject can come in the middle of the complete predicate. In the sentence below, the complete subject is in **boldface**. Part of the complete predicate is before it, and part is after it.

> In the early days of our history, **Benjamin Franklin** wanted the national bird of the United States to be a turkey, not an eagle.

Compound Subjects and Compound Predicates

Sometimes a verb can have more than one subject.

Jessica and Aaron took Jade for a walk.

Jessica and *Aaron* are called **compound subjects**. ("Compound" means two working together.)

Sometimes a subject can have more than one verb.

Jade laughed and played the whole day.

Laughed and *played* are called **compound verbs**.

Fragments and How to Fix Them

A group of words can begin with a capital letter, end with a period, question mark, or exclamation mark, and look like a sentence. But it isn't a sentence if it doesn't express a complete thought. Usually the subject or the predicate is missing. These words are called a **fragment** (a part of a sentence, but not the whole thing). A fragment can be short or long, as in the following sentence.

Strapping on his trusty parachute and jumping out the door of the high-flying plane into the frigid night air.

The old man with the long gray beard and the multi-colored freckles on his bulbous nose.

Plunked into the murky creek.

Since a fragment has missing parts, you have to fill in the missing parts to fix it.

Fragment (*the subject is missing*):

Whooping and hollering after winning the championship.

Fixed sentence:

My high school football team was whooping and hollering after winning the championship.

Fragment (*the predicate is missing*):

> A baboon with multi-colored feathers in its hair and large earrings shaped like pineapples.

Fixed sentence:

> A baboon with multi-colored feathers in its hair and large earrings shaped like pineapples was handing out free honey-roasted peanuts as people came into the circus.

Remember, a good sentence has a subject and a predicate, and it makes complete sense.

Clauses

A clause is a group of words that contains a subject and a verb. If the clause makes complete sense and can stand alone and be a sentence by itself, it's called a **main clause**.

> The moon rose at 7:18 tonight.

Other names for **main clause** are **principal clause** and **independent clause**. People use all three names for a clause that can be a sentence by itself.

If the clause cannot stand alone and express a complete thought, it's called a **dependent clause.** (It depends on another clause to make a whole sentence.)

> As I was looking out the car window, the moon rose at 7:18 tonight.

As I was looking out the car window does not express a complete thought and could not be a sentence by itself.

Another name for a **dependent clause** is a **subordinate clause**. People use the two names interchangeably.

34

Simple, Compound, and Complex Sentences

Simple Sentence

If a sentence is made up of one main (principal, independent) clause, it's called a **simple sentence**.

> He ran out into the street in his underwear.

Compound Sentence

If you put two or more main clauses together, you have a **compound sentence**.

> He was frightened by the strange noises coming from his closet, and he ran out into the street in his underwear.

That sentence is really two clauses that could each be a separate sentence. The clauses are related in meaning, and one is just as important as the other. They are connected by a comma plus a conjunction.

Complex Sentence

If you combine an independent (main, principal) clause with a dependent (subordinate) clause, you have a **complex sentence**. It doesn't matter which clause comes first.

> When he heard strange noises coming from his closet, he ran out into the street in his underwear.

> He ran out into the street in his underwear when he heard strange noises coming from his closet.

Run-On Sentences and How to Fix Them

If the main clauses are connected by just a comma, that's a **run-on sentence**, and that's not good. A comma is not strong enough punctuation to hold main clauses together.

> The rocket ship landed on Jupiter, the astronauts shouted, "Hooray!"

The main clauses in a compound sentence must be connected by a comma plus a conjunction or by a semicolon.

See *Conjunctions* on page 27 and *Semicolons* on page 91.

A run-on sentence can be fixed in several ways:

1. Add a conjunction after the comma.

*The rocket ship landed on Jupiter, **and** the astronauts shouted, "Hooray!"*

2. Connect the clauses with a semicolon.

The rocket ship landed on Jupiter; the astronauts shouted, "Hooray!"

3. Change one of the independent clauses to a dependent clause.

When the rocket ship landed on Jupiter, the astronauts shouted, "Hooray!"

4. Start a new sentence.

The rocket ship landed on Jupiter. The astronauts shouted, "Hooray!"

Try to avoid having too many short sentences in a row. Use a combination of short sentences and longer compound and complex sentences to make your writing more varied and interesting.

PARAGRAPHS

What Is a Paragraph?

Just as words go together to make sentences, sentences go together to make paragraphs. A paragraph is a group of sentences that all relate to the same thought or topic. The sentences move the main idea along.

A one-sentence paragraph would be dramatic or unexpected, especially if it came after several longer paragraphs.

And that was the last she ever heard from her brother's gerbil!

However, most paragraphs are about two to six sentences long. A paragraph with a lot of details could be longer.

How to Write a Good Paragraph

When you write a paragraph in an essay or in a research report, start with a topic sentence that states the main idea and tells what the paragraph is about in a general way. The sentences that follow should support that topic and add new facts, information, details, or examples. The last sentence usually sums up the main idea of the paragraph or restates it in different words.

Topic Sentence: states the main idea

Supporting Sentences: give details, examples, etc.

Last Sentence: sums up or restates the main idea

PARAGRAPHS

When to Start a New Paragraph

Start a new paragraph when you write about a new idea or a different aspect of the same idea. Start a new paragraph when the time, action, place, speaker, or characters change. You should also start a new paragraph if the one you're writing is starting to get too long.

See *Punctuating Direct Quotations* on page 90 for more about when to start a new paragraph.

My Birthday

My birthday this year was great! It was on a Saturday, so I could sleep late. My dad made my favorite breakfast: crispy waffles with tons of syrup. After breakfast, I helped my mom put together my new bike, and then I went to the ball game. I pitched for five innings and struck out the other team's three best players.

At night, we all went to Sloppy Pete's Pizza Palace, and I ordered a super special with pepperoni and sausage. It came with a birthday candle in it. Then I got to choose a movie with my friends. We saw <u>Dinosaur Monsters Eat the World!</u> My little brother kept his eyes shut through most of it. I hope all my birthdays are as great as this one.

Make sure that all the sentences work together to explain the same basic idea. If any sentence doesn't belong, cut it out. For example, the following sentence would not belong in the story about "My Birthday" even though it's about eating at a restaurant on someone's birthday because it's not about "my birthday."

Last year, on my Aunt Paula's birthday, we had Indian food.

The topic sentence is usually the first sentence, but sometimes, for variety, it could be at the end.

At "Cute Creatures," the giant cockatoo almost bit my nose. The turtle dove into its tank and splashed my new jacket. I almost stepped on the rabbit that was loose, the snake hissed at me, and a tiny puppy barked loudly in my ear when I nuzzled it. A trip to a pet store can sometimes be hazardous to your health.

Chapter 3
Spelling: Getting the Letters Right

WHY IS SPELLING SO IMPORTANT?

There are over 600,000 words in English, and each one of them has one correct spelling and many incorrect spellings. So you have a lot of chances to spell a word wrong.

Correct spelling is important to you because when you write a book report, a letter, an article for the school newspaper, a story, or even a note to your parents that you stick on the refrigerator, you want your readers to understand you clearly. Misspelled words can confuse your readers.

Besides, you don't want to be embarrassed by misspelled words. Too many wrong words in your writing can be mortifying.

WHAT ABOUT SPELL CHECKERS?

It's really important to learn the most important spelling rules, even if you have a spell checker on your computer. (Besides, you don't always write on a computer.)

Want proof? Below is a little story about a mother whose son is in trouble at school. If you read the story aloud, it will sound perfect. But if you look at it closely, you'll see that it actually contains 46 mistakes. And the spell checker missed every one of them! Find out why after you read the story.

> She took a peace of stationary out of her draw and rote two her sun's school.
>
> > Deer Principle,
> >
> > Eye due knot want two waist you're thyme. Aye herd my buoy did something that was knot aloud.
> >
> > Aisle bee inn too sea ewe at fore, sew pleas weight four me. Heal bee write their two, even if it reigns. Wee no yule bee fare with hymn when we meat yew.
> >
> > Buy.

Now here's that same story with all the mistakes corrected.

> She took a **piece** of **stationery** out of her **drawer** and **wrote to** her **son's** school.
>
> > **Dear Principal,**
> >
> > **I do not** want **to waste your time. I heard** my **boy** did something that was **not allowed.**
> >
> > **I'll be in to see you** at **four, so please wait for** me. **He'll be right there too,** even if it **rains. We know you'll be fair** with **him** when we **meet you.**
> >
> > **Bye**.

Why did the spell checker miss every mistake? Because the mistakes aren't spelling mistakes. They are homonyms (sometimes called homophones), words that sound the same as other words but have different spellings and meanings. Your spell checker can't correct homonyms because there's nothing wrong with their spelling.

For more on *Homonyms*, see page 97.

Vowels and Consonants
Before we get to the spelling rules, let's just make sure we get "vowels" and "consonants" straight. Remember that **a, e, i, o, u**, and sometimes **y** are the **vowels**. All the other letters are the **consonants**.

SPELLING

SEVENTEEN SUPER SPELLING RULES

1. Divide longer words into parts
2. The silent *e*. Drop it? Keep it?
3. Double the final consonant
4. Change *y* to *i*
5. *ie* or *ei* ?
6. When two vowels go walking
7. Plurals of nouns
8. Adding Prefixes
9. Adding Suffixes
10. Silent Letters
11. -able? or -ible?
12. Adding *k* to verbs ending with *c*
13. *-ful* has only one *l*
14. "*ough*" is tough!
15. Words with different spellings
16. Watch out for those first few letters
17. Use your dictionary or spell checker

1. Divide Longer Words into Parts

You'll sometimes have better luck spelling a long word correctly if you try to sound it out part by part, and then learn each part separately.

For instance, *superintendent*. Think of it as *super in ten dent*. Four short sounds are always easier to spell than one long one.

This plan won't work so well if the word has a totally weird spelling, especially at the beginning. But try it. It works pretty well if there are little words inside the bigger word. It will probably work with words like:

abundance	(a bun dance)	*handkerchief*	(hand ker chief)
amendment	(a mend ment)	*kindergarten*	(kin der gar ten)
attendance	(at ten dance)	*maintenance*	(main ten ance)
bungalow	(bung a low)	*nevertheless*	(nev er the less)
countenance	(count en ance)	*opportunity*	(op por tun i ty)
dormitory	(dorm i tor y)	*propaganda*	(prop a gan da)
enlargement	(en large ment)	*refrigerator*	(re frig er a tor)
extraordinary	(ex tra or din ar y)	*significant*	(sig ni fi cant)
fundamental	(fun da men tal)	*thermometer*	(ther mom e ter)
government	(gov ern ment)	*uniform*	(un i form)

See *Watch out for Those First Few Letters* on page 58.

41

2. The Silent *E*. Drop It? Keep It?

If an e isn't pronounced at the end of a word, drop it when you add a suffix that begins with a vowel (like -*ed*, -*ing*, -*age*, -*able*, -*ance*, -*al*, -*ible*, -*or* and -*ous*).

adventure	+ ous	= adventurous		force	+ ible	= forcible
arrive	+ al	= arrival		guide	+ ance	= guidance
dance	+ ed	= danced		love	+ able	= lovable
decorate	+ or	= decorator		store	+ age	= storage

The "drop the silent e" rule is used most often when you add -*ing* to a verb.

write	+ ing	= writing		become	+ ing	= becoming
come	+ ing	= coming		give	+ ing	= giving
dine	+ ing	= dining		change	+ ing	= changing
hope	+ ing	= hoping		judge	+ ing	= judging
scare	+ ing	= scaring		encourage	+ ing	= encouraging
argue	+ ing	= arguing		type	+ ing	= typing

Exceptions: As with many other rules, there are some exceptions to the "drop the silent e" rule. **Do not drop the silent e when the word ends with a soft -ge or soft -ce and you're adding a suffix that begins with -*ous* or -*able*.**

courage	+ ous	= courageous		salvage	+ able	= salvageable
outrage	+ ous	= outrageous		notice	+ able	= noticeable
advantage	+ ous	= advantageous		pronounce	+ able	= pronounceable
change	+ able	= changeable		peace	+ able	= peaceable
manage	+ able	= manageable		slice	+ able	= sliceable

A few verbs that end with a silent e do not drop the e because then they might be confused with other verbs.

For instance, the verb to *singe* usually means to burn the ends of your hair by touching it briefly to a flame. If you dropped the silent e when you added –**ing** to *singe*, people would think the word was *singing*. That would make for a very bizarre sentence:

> She was almost singing the ends of her eyelashes by leaning too close to the campfire.

So, *sing* + *ing* = *singing*, and *singe* + *ing* = *singeing*. And a person could be *singing* a song and *singeing* her eyelashes all in one sentence!

SPELLING

In the same way, a dressmaker is *dyeing* a dress green, not *dying* it. (A plant that you forget to water is dying.) And a person who really, really wants to change the color of her dress could be *dying* to be *dyeing* it.

singe	+ ing	=	singeing
eye	+ ing	=	eyeing
dye	+ ing	=	dyeing

Do not drop the silent e when you add −*ing* to four verbs that end with *-oe*.

hoe	+ ing	=	hoeing
toe	+ ing	=	toeing
canoe	+ ing	=	canoeing
shoe	+ ing	=	shoeing

It was a busy day on the farm. The farmer was **hoeing** the fields, the blacksmith was **shoeing** a horse, the girl was **canoeing** on the river, and I was **toeing** the line (obeying the rules).

Finally, here are two more exceptions to the "drop the silent e" rule, in case you ever need these words.

mile	+ age	=	mileage
acre	+ age	=	acreage

That takes care of the "drop the silent e" rule and its exceptions. Now here's when you do <u>not</u> drop the silent e: **Keep the silent e when you add a suffix that begins with a consonant: *-teen, -ty, -less, -ly, -ment, -ful,* etc.**

nine	+ teen	=	nineteen		sure	+ ly	=	surely
nine	+ ty	=	ninety		sincere	+ ly	=	sincerely
use	+ less	=	useless		immediate	+ ly	=	immediately
safe	+ ly	=	safely		definite	+ ly	=	definitely
arrange	+ ment	=	arrangement		manage	+ ment	=	management
care	+ ful	=	careful		use	+ ful	=	useful

Exceptions: Of course, there are some exceptions to this rule, too. (What would a rule be without exceptions?) Drop the silent e when adding a suffix that begins with a consonant in the following words.

nine	+ th	=	ninth	argue	+ ment =	argument
true	+ ly	=	truly	acknowledge	+ ment =	acknowledgment
due	+ ly	=	duly			

You can drop or keep the silent e in *judge* when you add -*ment*. Some dictionaries give both spellings. (Most dictionaries, however, give *judgment* as the preferred spelling.)

judge + ment = judgment or judgement

See *Words with Different Spellings* on page 57.

3. Double the Final Consonant

If a word ends with a single vowel and a single consonant, double the final consonant when you add a suffix that begins with a vowel (especially –*ed*, –*er*, and –*ing*).

Words that follow this rule end with letters like -*an*, -*am*, -*ap*, -*ar*, -*el*, -*er*, -*ep*, -*et*, -*ip*, -*ol*, -*op*, -*ot*, -*ow*, -*ub*, -*ug*, and -*ur*.

bar	+ ed	+ ing		=	barred, barring
compel	+ ed	+ ing		=	compelled, compelling
control	+ ed	+ ing		=	controlled, controlling
forget	+ ing			=	forgetting
occur	+ ed	+ ing		=	occurred, occurring
plan	+ ed	+ ing	+ er	=	planned, planning, planner
plot	+ ed	+ ing	+ er	=	plotted, plotting, plotter
prefer	+ ed	+ ing		=	preferred, preferring
slam	+ ed	+ ing		=	slammed, slamming
slap	+ ed	+ ing		=	slapped, slapping
scrub	+ ed	+ ing	+ er	=	scrubbed, scrubbing, scrubber
step	+ ed	+ ing		=	stepped, stepping
stop	+ ed	+ ing		=	stopped, stopping
tip	+ ed	+ ing	+ er	=	tipped, tipping, tipper
tug	+ ed	+ ing		=	tugged, tugging
swim	+ ing	+ er		=	swimming, swimmer
bag	+ age			=	baggage
big	+ est			=	biggest
control	+ able			=	controllable
forbid	+ en			=	forbidden
rebel	+ ion			=	rebellion
remit	+ ance			=	remittance

SPELLING

Exceptions: The words in the list on the opposite page are all one-syllable words or longer words where the accent falls on the last syllable. **Do not double the final consonant if the accent does not fall on the last syllable.**

In the words below, the accent is not on the last syllable, so the **final consonant is not doubled.**

happen	+ ed	+ ing		=	happened, happening
offer	+ ed	+ ing		=	offered, offering
sur**ren**der	+ ed	+ ing		=	surrendered, surrendering
snorkel	+ ed	+ ing		=	snorkeled, snorkeling
de**vel**op	+ ed	+ ing	+ er	=	developed, developing, developer
suffer	+ ed	+ ing	+ er	=	suffered, suffering, sufferer
borrow	+ ed	+ ing	+ er	=	borrowed, borrowing, borrower
travel	+ ed	+ ing	+ er	=	traveled, traveling, traveler
open	+ ed	+ ing		=	opened, opening, opener

4. Change Y to I

When you add *-es, -er, -est,* and *-ed* to a word that ends with a consonant and the letter *y*, change the *y* to *i*.

story	stories	lucky	luckier, luckiest
fam**i**ly	families	early	earlier, earliest
ene**my**	enemies	dirty	dirtier, dirtiest
la**dy**	ladies	dry	dries, dried
ba**by**	babies	busy	busier, busiest
ea**sy**	easier, easiest	hurry	hurries, hurried
hap**py**	happier, happiest	study	studies, studies
hea**vy**	heavier, heaviest	try	tries, tried

5. ie or ei?

There's a famous little poem that teachers and parents have been reciting for years that's supposed to help kids decide whether a word is spelled with *ie* or *ei*.

i before e

except after c

or when sounding like A

as in "neighbor" or "weigh"

Take the first line, for instance: *i before e*. All these words have *i before e*:

achieve	friend	piece
believe	pie	priest
brief	grief	retrieve
chief	lie	shield
field	niece	thief
fiend	patient	yield

The second line says: **except after c**. The following words have **e before i** because those letters come right after **c**.

ceiling	conceive	perceive
conceit	deceit	receipt
conceited	deceive	receive

The last two lines of the poem are **or when sounding like A / as in "neighbor" or "weigh."**

The following words all have an **A** sound that is spelled **ei**.

beige	neighbor	veil
deign	reign	vein
eighty	rein	weigh
freight	reindeer	weight
lei	skein	
neigh	sleigh	

Exceptions: It would be great if the poem worked 100% of the time and always helped you to decide whether to spell a word with *ie* or *ei*. But, there are exceptions to the poem. There are words that have *i before e*, even when they come after **c**:

an**ci**ent	finan**ci**er	spe**ci**es
defi**ci**ent	s**ci**entist	suffi**ci**ent
effi**ci**ent	so**ci**ety	

There are words that have **e** *before* **i**, and they don't come after **c**, and they don't sound like **A**.

caff**ei**ne	h**ei**ght	sh**ei**k
cod**ei**ne	kal**ei**doscope	sl**ei**ght
counterf**ei**t	l**ei**sure	sov**ei**reign
either	n**ei**ther	st**ei**n
for**ei**gn	prot**ei**n	th**ei**r
forf**ei**t	s**ei**smologist	w**ei**rd
h**ei**fer	s**ei**ze	

So, what should you do with a rule that has so many exceptions? You should learn the poem, but be familiar with the exceptions, too.

6. When Two Vowels Go Walking

Your first or second grade teacher probably taught you the following rule, and it's still a good one: **When two vowels go walking, the first vowel does the talking.**

This rule doesn't work all the time, but it works with *ai*, *ea*, *oe*, and *oa* words. And there are a lot of those.

Think of a *steamboat*. The letters *ea* in *steam* sound like the first letter, *e*. The letters *oa* in *boat* sound like the first letter, *o*. Many words follow this rule, including the following:

ai words		*ea* words		*oe* words	*oa* words
aid	sail	beam	peat	aloe	bloat
aim	tail	beat	pearl	doe	boast
bail	vail	bleat	pleat	floe	boat
bait	vain	cheat	preach	foe	cloak
fail	waif	cleat	real	hoe	coach
fair	wail	cream	ream	Joe	coal
gain	wait	crease	release	oboe	coast
gait	braid	deal	scream	roe	coat
ail	brain	defeat	seal	sloe	croak
jail	chain	dream	seam	toe	float
laid	claim	eager	seat	woe	foal
lain	drain	feat	shear		foam
lair	flail	flea	sneak		goal
maid	frail	gleam	speak		goat
mail	grail	grease	squeak		groan
main	grain	heal	squeal		Joan
nail	Maine	heat	steal		load
paid	plain	heave	steam		loam
pail	quail	leak	streak		loan
pain	quaint	lease	stream		moan
raid	stain	meal	team		moat
rail	trail	mean	treat		poach
rain	train	meat	veal		roach
	wraith	neat	weak		road
		peak	wheat		roam
		peal	wreath		roast
			zeal		shoal
					soak
					throat
					toad
					toast

7. Plurals of Nouns

"Singular" means just one person, place, thing, or idea. "Plural" means two or more. **Most nouns just add the letter *s* when you make them plural.**

Singular (just one) **Plural** (more than one)

one joystick	three joystick**s**
a basketball	a bag of basketball**s**
this shoe	this pair of shoe**s**
the kid	a room full of kid**s**

If all the nouns in English did that, spelling plurals would be easy. But, of course, there are some nouns that change their spellings when they become plural. They fall into certain categories (see the lists of irregular nouns below), and unless you are going to use only singular nouns in all of your writing, you need to learn them.

Change the end of the word

child	children
ox	oxen

Change *f* and *fe* to *ve* and add *s*

shelf	shelves	loaf	loaves	sheaf	sheaves
elf	elves	calf	calves	life	lives
thief	thieves	wolf	wolves	knife	knives
leaf	leaves	half	halves	wife	wives

Exception: fife, fifes

Add *s* to words ending with a vowel and *o*

cameo	cameos	radio	radios	taboo	taboo
cuckoo	cuckoos	rodeo	rodeos	tattoo	tattoos
igloo	igloos	shampoo	shampoos	video	videos

Add *es* to most words ending with a consonant and *o*

echo	echoes	potato	potatoes	veto	vetoes
hero	heroes	tomato	tomatoes		

Exceptions: burros, broncos, condos, gismos (gizmos), photos, torsos

Add *s* to words that end with *o* and have to do with music

alto	altos	piano	piano	soprano	sopranos
cello	cellos	banjo	banjos	solo	solos
mezzo	mezzos	piccolo	piccolos	tango	tangos

Some words that end with *o* have more than one plural spelling (-*os* or –*oes*)

domino	dominos, dominoes	motto	mottos, mottoes
gazebo	gazebos, gazeboes	tornado	tornados, tornadoes
halo	halos, haloes	volcano	volcano, volcanoes
mosquito	mosquito, mosquitoes	zero	zeros, zeroes

When a word ends in *y*, change the *y* to *i* and add *es* when the letter before the *y* is a consonant

baby	babies	buggy	buggies
lady	ladies	puppy	puppies
berry	berries	guppy	guppies
belly	bellies		

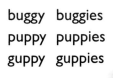

Exceptions: Proper nouns that end with a consonant and **y** (just add **s**) to become plural.

Germany	Germanys
Sally	Sallys
Kennedy	Kennedys

Change the middle of the word

tooth	teeth	foot	feet
mouse	mice	tooth	teeth
louse	lice	man	men
goose	geese		

Exceptions:

talisman	talismans	ottoman	ottomans

Family members

mother-in-law	mothers-in-law	father-in-law	fathers-in-law
brother-in-law	brothers-in-law	sister-in-law	sisters-in-law

Add es to words that end with the letters s, ss, x, ch, and sh

box	boxes	gas	gases	brush	brushes
kiss	kisses	church	churches	watch	watches

Words that don't change from singular to plural

moose	moose	sheep	sheep	bison	bison
deer	deer	swine	swine	series	series

Words with more than one way to spell the plural

fish	fish or fishes
hippopotamus	hippopotami or hippopotamuses
octopus	octopi or octopuses
appendix	appendixes or appendices
antenna	bug antennae or tv antennas
dwarf	dwarfs or dwarves
wharf	wharfs or wharves
staff	staves (sticks or in music), staffs (people)
scarf	scarfs or scarves
bus	buses or busses
cactus	cacti or cactuses
hoof	hoofs or hooves
rhinoceros	rhinoceros or rhinoceroses

Words from Latin and Greek

datum	data	medium	media
basis	bases	alga	algae
bacterium	bacteria	crisis	crises
die	dice	alumnus	alumni

8. Adding Prefixes

When you add a prefix to a word, just add it. Don't change the spelling of either the prefix or the word.

This is the easiest spelling rule of them all. A prefix is a little part of a word, usually just two to four letters, that you put at the beginning of a word. If you follow the rule above, you will never misspell "misspell," which has two s's: one at the end of *mis* and one at the beginning of *spell*.

A prefix always changes the meaning of a word.

Prefix	Base Word	Final Spelling
anti-	war	antiwar
auto-	biography	autobiography
bi-	cycle	bicycle
co-	operate	cooperate
dis-	appoint	disappoint
il-	legal	illegal
im-	mature	immature
inter-	national	international
ir-	responsible	irresponsible
mid-	term	midterm
mis-	understand	misunderstand
multi-	purpose	multipurpose
non-	essential	nonessential
pre-	view	preview
re-	appear	reappear
re-	union	reunion
tele-	scope	telescope
un-	usual	unusual
un-	certain	uncertain
under-	ground	underground

The only case when a prefix does not change the meaning of the word it's attached to is *inflammable*, which you might think means "not flammable." Surprise! *Inflammable* has exactly the same meaning as *flammable*: easily set on fire and able to burn quickly.

Sometimes, if the last letter of the prefix and the first letter of the base word are both vowels, a hyphen goes between them to make the word easier to read. This is especially true if the vowels are the same. If you're not sure about the hyphen, check your dictionary.

pro-education   co-author   anti-inflation   pre-election

Also, use a hyphen to avoid confusion between words.

recount: tell a story   *re-count*: count again
recollect: to remember   *re-collect*: to collect again
recover: to get back   *re-cover*: to cover again

Before I **recount** my adventures with the pirates, let me **re-count** the number of gold coins in my treasure box.

See *Hyphens* on page 87.

9. Adding Suffixes

Suffixes are little parts of words that go on the ends of other words, (like *-ly, -ness, -ful,* and many more). Usually suffixes change the meanings of words or add information to them.

When you add a suffix to a base word, in most cases you just add it. Don't change the spelling of the suffix or the base (unless there's a silent e at the end of the base word or you have to double the final consonant). Examples of these exceptions are *argument* and *slammed*.

Base	Suffix	Final Spelling
adult	-hood	adulthood
appoint	-ment	appointment
back	-ward	backward
beautiful	-ly	beautifully
character	-ize	characterize
cheerful	-ness	cheerfulness
child	-like	childlike
child	-ish	childish
count	-ess	countess
fear	-less	fearless
fraud	-ulent	fraudulent
free	-dom	freedom
govern	-ess	governess
hope	-ful	hopeful
paint	-er	painter
pilgrim	-age	pilgrimage
quarrel	-some	quarrelsome
swordsman	-ship	swordsmanship

See *The Silent E. Drop It? Keep It?* on page 42 and *Double the Final Consonant* on page 44.

53

If would be tough enough to spell English words if you could pronounce all the letters in all the words. But many words contain letters that you don't even sound out when you say them. You still have to put them in when you write them, however. Here are some of the most common words with silent letters.

align, benign, design, sign

answer

balk, calk, chalk, stalk, talk, walk

bright, flight, light, might, night, right, sight, tight

column

Connecticut

could, should, would

cupboard

debris

dumb, thumb, plumber

gnome

handkerchief

handsome

high, nigh, sigh, thigh

island

knave, knew, knot, know

listen

often

salmon

subtle

thought, brought, taught

Wednesday

wrap, wreck, write, wrong

For more on silent letters, see *Watch out for Those First Few Letters* on page 58.

11. -able? or -ible?

Hundreds of words in English end with the letters -able or –ible, and there's no good rule that will help you decide which ending to put on which word. I know it's not sens**ible** to have no rule. Really incred**ible**! Unbeliev**able**. And trying to spell words like these can be formid**able** and make you miser**able**. You might think that these words are horr**ible**. Detest**able**. But you are cap**able** of spelling them correctly. You have to. They're unavoid**able**. And it's not accept**able** to spell them wrong. It's inexcus**able**. It's definitely poss**ible** to spell them right. The best thing to do is become familiar with the valu**able** lists below and always check your dictionary or spell checker when in doubt. That's an attain**able** goal.

-able	-able	-ible	-ible
acceptable	inexcusable	accessible	inflexible
amiable	inflammable	combustible	intangible
attainable	invaluable	contemptible	invincible
avoidable	justifiable	corruptible	invisible
believable	miserable	credible	permissible
capable	mutable	crucible	plausible
changeable	notable	edible	possible
conceivable	passable	flexible	responsible
delectable	portable	forcible	reversible
deplorable	presentable	horrible	sensible
desirable	probable	illegible	tangible
detestable	reliable	impossible	terrible
immovable	respectable	incredible	unintelligible
incurable	untouchable	indelible	visible

12. Adding *k* to Verbs Ending with *c*

When you add -*ing* or -*ed* to some verbs that end with *c*, you have to add *k* first.

So, first you *picnic* on the grass. Then you are *picnicking* on the grass. And finally you *picnicked* on the grass. Here is a list of verbs that end in *c* and add *k* before -*ing* and -*ed*.

Now we . . .	We are . . .	Then we . . .
frolic	frolicking	frolicked
mimic	mimicking	mimicked
panic	panicking	panicked
picnic	picnicking	picnicked
traffic	trafficking	trafficked

13. -*ful* Has Only One *l*

When you add the suffix -*ful* to a word, make sure it has only one *l*. Since "beautiful" means "full of beauty" and "powerful" means "full of power," it is natural to think that these words should end with -*full*. But that is not so. The correct suffix is spelled -*ful*.

The only word in the English language that ends with *full* is "full." Below is a list of the most common words that end with -*ful*.

armful	cupful	gleeful	mindful	tactful
artful	doubtful	graceful	painful	tasteful
awful	dreadful	grateful	peaceful	teaspoonful
bashful	dutiful	handful	pitiful	thimbleful
beautiful	earful	harmful	plentiful	trustful
blissful	eventful	hateful	powerful	unlawful
boastful	eyeful	helpful	shameful	wasteful
bountiful	faithful	hopeful	sinful	wishful
capful	fanciful	hurtful	skillful	woeful
careful	fateful	joyful	sorrowful	wonderful
cheerful	fearful	masterful	spiteful	worshipful
colorful	forceful	merciful	tablespoonful	youthful

14. "Ough" Is Tough!

One group of letters needs a section all its own: **ough**.
Probably no other combination of five letters in the whole
English language has so many different possible pronunciations,
and not one of them is "o-ug-huh," as someone might think.

"uff"	"ow"	"off"	"oh"	"aw"	"oo"
enough	bough	cough	although	bought	through
rough	drought	trough	borough	brought	
tough	plough	hiccough	dough	fought	
		(hiccup)	furlough	sought	
			thorough	thought	
			though	wrought	

Now you know how tough "ough" is.

"Slough"
can be pronounced three different
ways depending on what the word means.

Slough ("**ow**"): a suburb of London, England

slough ("**oo**" and "**ow**"): A depression, usually filled
with deep mud; a stagnant swamp or marsh.

slough ("**uff**"): The dead outer skin shed by
a reptile or an amphibian.

15. Words with Different Spellings

Andrew Jackson (1767-1845), the seventh president of the United States,
was once trying to write an important paper, and he was having trouble
with his spelling. It was reported that he cried out
angrily, "It's a poor mind that can think of only
one way to spell a word."

Back on page 39, at the beginning of this section on spelling, I said that there was only
one right way to spell a word. That's true for
about 99.9% of all the words in the English
language. (Sorry, President Jackson.)

But there are a few words that have two correct spellings. In your dictionary, both accepted spellings will be given with the words "also" or "or" between them.

Many words in English that end with **-or** in the United States end with **-our** in Britain, another big country that speaks English as its native language. In your dictionary, for instance, *colour* may be identified as "Chiefly British. Variant of *color*." ("Variant" means a different, acceptable spelling.)

So in the United States, spell the following words with **-or** at the end:

behavior	endeavor	humor	odor
candor	flavor	labor	parlor
clamor	harbor	misdemeanor	rumor
color	honor	neighbor	vigor

Don't be surprised, however, if you sometimes see these same words spelled with **-our** at the end, especially in a book or an article by a British writer. (Words that end with **-ize** or **-er** in the United States are sometimes spelled with **-ise** and **-re** in Britain. Examples: apolog**ize**, apolog**ise**; cent**er**, cent**re**.)

Other words that have two acceptable spellings are:

catalogue, catalog

judgement, judgment

theater, theatre

cancellation, cancelation

16. Watch out for Those First Few Letters

Sometimes you have a better chance of spelling a word right if you can figure out the first few letters. Then at least you'll know where to look in your dictionary.

Since so many English words come from foreign languages, and since there are a lot of silent letters in English, the first few letters of many words are really tricky. The lists below should help you with some of the trickiest.

c sounds like **s** at the beginning of words that begin with **ce-**, **ci-**, and **cy-** like

ceiling	censor	ceramic	cinch	cyanide
celebrate	censorship	cereal	cinder	cycle
celebrity	cent	ceremony	cinema	cyclone
celery	centennial	certain	circle	cyclorama
celestial	centigrade	certificate	circus	cygnet
cellar	centimeter	certify	citizen	cylinder
cellophane	centipede	cider	citrus	cymbal
cellular	central	cipher	civilian	cypress
cement	century	cigar	civilization	cyst

c sounds like **k** at the beginning of all words that begin with **ca-**, **co-**, or **cu-**: **capital**, **coconut**, **cube**, etc.

ch sounds like **k** at the beginning of words like

character	chlorine	chorus
chemical	choral	Christmas
chemistry	chord	chrome

ch sounds like **sh** at the beginning of words like

chalet	charade	chauffeur	chiffon
champagne	charlatan	chef	chivalry
chandelier	chateau	chic	chute

g sounds like **j** at the beginning of words like

gelatin	genetic	geometric	gibberish
gem	genie	geranium	gigantic
gender	genius	gerbil	giraffe
gene	gentle	germ	gym
general	gentleman	German	gymnastic
generator	genuine	gesture	gypsy
generosity	geography	giant	gyroscope

gh sounds like ***g*** at the beginning of words like

Ghana	gherkin	ghost
ghastly	ghetto	ghoul

kn sounds like ***n*** at the beginning of words like

knack	knickerbockers	knot
knapsack	knife	knothole
knave	knight	know
knead	knit	knowledge
knee	knob	known
kneel	knock	Knoxville
knell	knoll	knuckle

ph sounds like ***f*** at the beginning of words like

phantom	phenomenal	philosophy	physics
pharmacist	Philadelphia	phobia	phone
pharmacy	philanthropy	Phoenix	phonics
Pharaoh	philharmonic	phrase	phony
phase	Phillip	physical	photocopy
pheasant	philosopher	physician	photography

ps sounds like ***s*** at the beginning of words like

psalm	psoriasis	psychic
pseudonym	psychiatrist	psychology

qu sounds like ***kw*** at the beginning of words like

quack	quarter	quilt
quail	queen	quit
quake	quench	quite
quality	question	quiz
quarrel	quick	quota
quart	quiet	quote

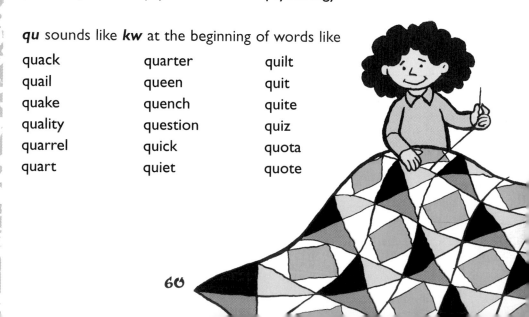

squ sounds like *sk* at the beginning of words like

squabble	square	squeal	squirm
squad	squash	squeamish	squirrel
squadron	squat	squeeze	squirt
squall	squaw	squelch	squish
squalor	squawk	squib	
squander	squeak	squint	

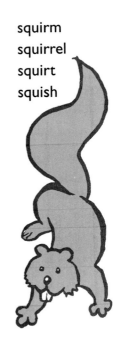

wh sounds like *h* at the beginning of words like

who	whom	whose	who's

wh sounds like *w* at the beginning of words like

whack	whether	whisker
whacky	which	whiskey
whale	whiff	whisper
wharf	whiffle	whistle
what	while	white
wheat	whim	whittle
where	whimper	whiz
wheedle	whip	whoops
wheeze	whirl	whoosh
wheel	whirlpool	whopper
when	whirr	why

wr sounds like *r* at the beginning of words like

wrack	wren	wrinkle
wrap	wrench	wrist
wrangle	wrestle	write
wreath	wretched	wrong
wreck	wriggle	wrote
wreckage	wring	wrung

17. Use Your Dictionary or Spell Checker

When you are writing something and you come to a word that you are not sure how to spell, you can do one of three things:

1. Try to spell it the best you can. Take a wild guess. You might actually get it right. Or you might end up with a sentence like *"It wuz a kold and winndy nite."*

2. Shout out to the nearest intelligent person, "How do you spell *sarcophagus?*" and hope that he or she is a better speller than you are.

Of course, your best bet is

3. Look the word up in your dictionary, or if you are on your computer, run it by the spell checker. (Be careful of homonyms! See page 97.)

Don't be a spell wrecker. Be a spell checker!

Make this your slogan for better spelling:

When in doubt, Get your dictionary out!

SPELLING

Chapter 4
Capitalization

Capital letters are very handy. They tell us when sentences begin. They identify the names of specific people, places, and things. They're helpful in other ways too. Here's when to use capital letters and when not to.

ALWAYS CAPITALIZE

The First Word of a Sentence

Giraffes would make cute pets if they could fit in the house.

The First Word of a Direct Quote

I told my teacher, "**M**y pet giraffe ate my homework," but she didn't believe me.

Exceptions: Do not capitalize the first word in an indirect quotation.

I told my teacher that my pet giraffe had eaten my homework, but she didn't believe me.

The First Word of Each Line of Poetry

TO MY BABY BROTHER, WITH LOVE

On my cookie, you may nibble;

On my drawings, you may scribble;

With these things I will not quibble,

But on my homework, do not dribble.

Thank you.

ALWAYS CAPITALIZE

The Pronoun I

I took the bus, and I went to my grandmother's house, and I helped her paint the living room, and I practiced karate with her, and I walked her alligator, and I jogged with her around the park, and I was exhausted.

Exceptions: Do not capitalize the other pronouns (*you, he, she, it, we, they, me, him, her, us, them, my, mine, your, yours, his, hers, its, our, ours, their,* and *theirs*) unless they are the first words in a sentence, title, etc.

See *Pronouns* on page 26.

Names of Specific People

Karen, David, Jennifer, George Washington, Pookey

Exceptions: Do not capitalize "man," "woman," "boy," "girl," and general words that indicate kinds of people without giving their specific names.

Names of Specific Places

Chelsea, MA	Brooklyn	Mississippi River	Asia
Pacific Ocean	California	Rocky Mountains	Central Park

Exceptions: Do not capitalize general place words like "city," "state," "mountain," "river," and "park" without the specific names in front.

Specific Buildings, Monuments, and Sites

Lincoln Memorial	Statue of Liberty
Golden Gate Bridge	the Kremlin
Empire State Building	Eiffel Tower
the Taj Mahal	Buckingham Palace

Exceptions: Do not capitalize "building," "statue," "tower," and general words like those without the specific proper names in front. Also, do not capitalize the word "the" in front of specific buildings or sites unless it is the first word in the sentence.

We took a tour of the White House, but the president wasn't in. So we went to the Washington Monument to see if Washington was there.

64

CAPITALIZATION

ALWAYS CAPITALIZE

Organizations and Institutions

Chamber of Commerce

Smithsonian Institution

National Football League

Library of Congress

Salvation Army

Better Business Bureau

Exceptions: Do not capitalize general words like "library," "institute," and "society" without the specific names in front.

Sports Teams

Atlanta Braves   Orlando Magic   Tennessee Titans

Exceptions: Do not capitalize general words like "team," "club," or "group" without the specific names.

Schools and Colleges

Columbia Prep School

Brooklyn College

Tufts University

State University of New York at New Paltz

Exceptions: Do not capitalize "school," "college," "university" and general words like those without the proper names in front.

Proper Adjectives

French poodle, French fries, French horn, Chinese food, German measles, Italian fashions, Japanese technology, Indian restaurant, Russian dances, Swiss cheese, Belgian lace, American economy

Proper adjectives are made from proper nouns.

See *Proper Nouns* on page 16.

ALWAYS CAPITALIZE

Initials That Are Part of Someone's Name

C. S. Lewis, Harry **S** Truman, John **F.** Kennedy,
F.D.R. (Franklin Delano Roosevelt), **J. K.** Rowling

Official Titles or Positions When Used with Names

General Jones, **C**aptain Kilmer, **P**resident Bush,
King Tut, **P**rime **M**inister Gerson

Exceptions: Do not capitalize "captain," "general,"
"ambassador," and similar words without the proper
names attached.

Family Members When Used with Their Names

Uncle **G**eorge, **A**unt **R**ozzie, **G**randpa **J**ake, **C**ousin **C**indy

Exceptions: Do not capitalize "uncle," "aunt," "grandma," and general
words like those without the specific names attached.

Mom and Dad When Used As If They Were Names

She told **M**om that **D**ad had said to tell her that she should meet him
where he had told her to. Understand?

Exceptions: Do not capitalize "my mom" or "my dad" or just "mom"
and "dad" when not being used as if they were the names of the mother and father.

My mom and her dad used to go to college together.

Family Members When Used as Nouns of Direct Address

And now, **M**om, **D**ad, **G**randma, and **G**randpa, sit down and listen
because I have some astounding news to tell you.

See *Noun of Direct Address* on page 19.

The Days of the Week

Tuesday, **T**hursday, **S**aturday, etc.

ALWAYS CAPITALIZE

The Months of the Year

February, April, July, August, etc.

The First Word in the Salutation (Greeting) of a Friendly Letter

My dear employees,

Hi, everyone,

Dearest pal,

Dear friend,

The First, Last, and All Important Words in the Salutation (Greeting) of a Business Letter

Dear Customer Relations Department:

Dear Public Safety Commissioner:

Dear Chairman of the Board:

The First Word in the Closing of a Letter

Yours truly,

Best wishes,

Sincerely yours,

Warmest regards,

Respectfully and gratefully,

Farewell for now,

The First, Last, and All the Main Words in Titles Of

books – Harry Potter and the Goblet of Fire

movies – The Lord of the Rings

songs – Happy Birthday

plays or musicals – Beauty and the Beast

magazines – Time for Kids

newspapers – The Boston Globe

TV shows – Wild Animal Adventures

Exceptions: Do not capitalize small words in a title like "a," "an," "the," "in," or "to" unless they're the first or last words.

ALWAYS CAPITALIZE

School Subjects

When they are the names of languages or specific courses listed in the school catalog

French Literature

Psychology for Beginners

Advanced Biology

Introduction to Swahili

World History II

Mastering Mathematics

Exceptions: Do not capitalize subjects that are not the names of languages or specific courses: mathematics, geography, history, science, etc.

The First Word of Each Line of an Outline

I. The World's Weirdest People
   A. Weird Men
      1. Appearance
      2. Actions
      3. Clothing
   B. Weird Women
      1. Names
      2. Hairdos
      3. Occupations

Geographic Locations

When they refer to specific areas on the map

She was born in the East, moved to the West when she was nine, traveled throughout the Northwest after college, and finally settled in the South. She's been around!

Exceptions: Do not capitalize "north," "east," "south," "west," etc., when they mean directions, not locations.

I was supposed to drive three miles south and then turn west; instead I drove eight miles north and then turned east. No wonder I was late.

ALWAYS CAPITALIZE

National Holidays

Thanksgiving, Father's Day, Mother's Day, Labor Day, Memorial Day, Washington's Birthday, Martin Luther King Day, New Year's Day

Religious Holidays

Christmas, Easter, Idul Fitr, Rosh Hashanah, Saint Patrick's Day

Local Holidays, Festivals, and Special Events

Young Authors Conference, Reading Rodeo,
Winter Wonderland, Fall Festival, Back-to-School Fair,
Kiddie Carnival, Summer Street Fair

Exceptions: Do not capitalize words like "festival," "jubilee," and "carnival," when they don't have specific names with them.

Races, Nationalities, and Religions

Caucasian, Semitic, Belgian, Italian, Spanish, Africans, Arabic, Christians, Jews, Asians, Muslims

Languages

French, Hebrew, Japanese, Latin, Greek, Russian

Historical Periods, Documents, and Events

the Great Depression

the Battle of Bunker Hill

Declaration of Independence

the Vietnam War

the Renaissance

the Middle Ages

Exceptions: Do not capitalize general words like "war," "battle," or "treaty" without specific names.

ALWAYS CAPITALIZE

Deities, Gods

God, **S**avior, **B**uddha, **J**ehovah, **A**llah

Exceptions: Do not capitalize the words "god" or "goddess" used in a general way.

People in ancient times believed that gods and goddesses could punish them if they were bad.

The Word *Bible* and All Books of the Bible

Bible, **G**enesis, **S**criptures

Religious Books

the **K**oran, the **T**orah, the **N**ew **T**estament

The Names of the Planets

Mercury, **V**enus, **M**ars, **J**upiter

Exceptions: Do not capitalize "sun" and "moon," and sometimes "earth." Capitalize "Earth" only when it refers to the third planet from the sun, our specific planet. When "earth" means dirt or soil, it is not capitalized.

The First Word in a Long Sentence After a Colon

There was a sign on the front door of the school: **T**here is no school today because the principal has gone fishing!

Exceptions: Do not capitalize the first word in a list after a colon.

Stuff to take to the party: pretzels, my goldfish, CD's, my favorite pillow, and jelly-flavored toothpaste.

Abbreviations of Titles After Someone's Name

John Smith, **J**r.   Mortimore Snobly, **S**r.

Wellman Sickly, **M.D.**   Henry Brainy, **Ph.D**

ALWAYS CAPITALIZE

The Postal Abbreviations for All the States

NY   MA   FL   GA   KY   TX   RI   WY   CA

A.M. and P.M.

A.M. (ante meridian, before noon) and **P.M.** (post meridian, after noon) can be capitalized or not. People do it both ways. It's your choice, but once you decide, try to do it the same way all the time.

A.D. and B.C.

Julius Caesar was assassinated in 44 **B.C.**

In **A.D.** 1492, Columbus set sail over the ocean blue.

> Note that A.D. comes before the year and B.C. comes after the year.

Names of Products

Nintendo games, **N**ike sneakers, **C**heerios, **K**leenex tissues

Exceptions: Do not capitalize general words like "sneakers," "cereal," "tissues," and "aspirin" that are not brand names.

Names of Companies

Sony **C**orporation, **G**eneral **M**otors, **K**ellogg **C**ompany

Do Not Capitalize the Seasons of the Year

spring, summer, fall, autumn, winter

Exceptions: If the name of the season is the first word in a sentence or a word in a title or part of the name of a local holiday, it should be capitalized.

My favorite poem is "**S**pring Has Sprung."

Decorations for the Super **S**ummer Carnival were great.

Winter is harsh in the Arctic regions. Ask a polar bear.

Chapter 5
Punctuation

WHY YOU NEED PROPER PUNCTUATION

Sentences and paragraphs are important, but without proper punctuation, they would be very difficult to read. Punctuation marks are like little road signs that tell you when to slow down, pause, and stop as you read. They help writers show their feelings and get their messages across clearly.

So, it's very important for you to use punctuation correctly. Otherwise your writing might be confusing. And what reader wants to be confused?

APOSTROPHES

Contractions

A contraction is a word you make by putting two or more words together and leaving out one or more letters. An apostrophe takes the place of the missing letter(s) in a contraction.

Here are some contractions that you use every day.

aren't	he'd	might've	they'll	who'd
can't	he'll	mustn't	they're	would've
couldn't	he's	needn't	they've	who'll
could've	I'd	shouldn't	we're	who's
didn't	I'll	she'd	wasn't	won't
doesn't	I'm	she'll	we'd	wouldn't
don't	isn't	she's	we'll	you've
hadn't	it's	that's	who's	you'd
hasn't	I've	there's	weren't	you'll
haven't	let's	they'd	we've	you're

73

The 've at the end of *should've*, *could've*, and *would've* always stands for *have*, never for *of*. For instance, *should've* always means *should have*, never *should of*.

You're means *you are*. **Your** means *belongs to you*.

> You're wrong if you think that your smelly dog is going to sleep in my bed.

It's stands for two words: *it is* or *it has*. **Its** means *belongs to it*.

> It's eating its dinner. (It is eating the dinner that belongs to it.)

Let's always means *let us*. **Lets** is the present tense of the verb *to let*.

> Sometimes she lets us eat bugs, so let's ask her if we can do it today.

Who's is a contraction for *who is* or *who has*. **Whose** means *belongs to whom*.

> Whose mess is this, and who's going to clean it up? (Who does this mess belong to, and who is going to clean it up?)

Possessive Nouns

Use apostrophes in all possessive nouns.

One of the jobs that nouns do in sentences is show possession or owner-ship. Every possessive noun must have an apostrophe. Sometimes it comes before the s and sometimes it comes after it. How do you know when to use 's and when to use s' ? It's easier than you think.

Singular Possessive Nouns

If the noun is singular, add 's to make it possessive.

It doesn't matter what the last letter of the singular noun is. It could be s or even ss. Just add 's to all singular nouns to make them show ownership.

> Dennis**'s** painting ladder
> the chipmunk**'s** nuts
> my boss**'s** lampshade
> the girl**'s** helicopter

There is one possible exception to this rule: when you make the names of people from ancient literature or the Bible possessive. If their names end with s, you can add either 's or just an apostrophe: Moses' orders, Jesus' sermon, Aeneas' ship, Odysseus' bow, Hercules' feats. If the name ends with any letter besides s, follow the regular rule for singular possessive nouns: Add 's.

Plural Possessive Nouns

If the noun is plural and you want it to show possession, look at the last letter. It will either be s, or it won't be. If the last letter of a plural noun is s, add just an apostrophe to make it possessive.

> the baseball players**'** uniforms
>
> the musician**s'** instruments
>
> the Leong**s'** new home
>
> the elephant**s'** watering hole

If the last letter of a plural noun is not s, add 's to make it possessive.

Most plural nouns end with s, but there are some irregular nouns that don't. Here are a few.

> the women**'s** briefcases
>
> the mice**'s** tricks
>
> the fathers-in-law**'s** gifts

Remember:

- Every possessive noun must have an apostrophe.

- All singular possessive nouns end with 's.

- If the last letter of a plural noun is s, just add an apostrophe to make it possessive.

- If the last letter of a plural noun is not s, add 's to make it possessive.

Plurals of Letters, Signs, Words, and Symbols

Use 's to make letters, signs, words, and symbols plural.

> How many a**'s** are there in Afghanistan?
>
> Don't put too many !**'s** at the end of your sentences, or you'll sound too hysterical.
>
> Instead of using so many *very***'s** in your story, try other adverbs like *extremely* or *intensely*.
>
> She drew ☺ **'s** all over her bedroom wall.

Plurals of Numbers and Decades

You can add 's or just plain s to make numbers and decades plural.

Choose one way, and do it that way all the time.

> The **2's** have nap time now, but the **3's** and **4's** can eat their snacks.

> Her most productive years as a snake charmer and mermaid imperson-ator were in the mid-1920**'s**.

> I forgot that his address has two **5s**, so I got lost.

> From the 1940**s** to the 1970**s**, the number of televisions in this country increased tremendously.

Apostrophes are really important when you make **letters** plural to avoid confusion in a sentence like:

> **Mississippi** is spelled with four is, four ss, and two ps.

See how much easier it is to read with the apostrophes:

> **Mississippi** is spelled with four i's, four s's, and two p's.

However, you don't always have to use apostrophes when you make **numbers** plural. See the sample sentences to the left.

BRACKETS

USE BRACKETS TO ADD YOUR OWN WORDS TO WORDS YOU ARE QUOTING.

> "We hold these truths to be self-evident, that all men [and all women, too, if you ask me] are created equal."
>
> —The Declaration of Independence

USE BRACKETS AROUND YOUR WORDS THAT REPLACE SOMEONE ELSE'S WORDS THAT YOU CUT OUT TO MAKE A QUOTATION SHORTER.

Original version:

Dear Editor:

I am so distressed that the city is going to take over our community garden, that when the bulldozers come to knock down the beeches, birches, cedars, cherries, chestnuts, maples, oaks, pines, and poplars, I'm going to chain myself to the gate and not let them in.

Sincerely,

The Leaf Lady

Shortened version with brackets around one word that was inserted to replace ten words that were deleted:

Dear Editor:

I am so distressed that the city is going to take over our community garden, that when the bulldozers come to knock down the ... [trees], I'm going to chain myself to the gate and not let them in.

Sincerely,

The Leaf Lady

See *Ellipses* on page 85 to see what the three dots in the letter above mean.

USE BRACKETS AROUND "SIC" TO KEEP SOMEONE'S MISTAKE WHEN YOU QUOTE HIS OR HER WORDS

"Sic" is a Latin word that means "just so." When you quote someone who has made a mistake, and you are not going to correct the mistake in the quote, put "sic" in brackets after the mistake. That way the reader will know that what comes before [sic] is spelled wrong or is an error of fact.

The boy wrote that the song begins, "My country 'tis of thee, sweet land of liver tea [sic], of thee I sing."

Some people put stage directions in brackets when they write the script of a play. The brackets separate what the actor says from what he or she does.

Roslyn: [stomping her foot on the floor] Keep those pigs out of my kitchen!

COLONS

USE A COLON AFTER A FULL SENTENCE THAT INTRODUCES A LIST

For your geography test, memorize the names and locations of the five longest rivers in the world: Nile (Africa), Amazon (South America), Yangtze (Asia), Huang Ho (Asia), and Congo (Africa).

For special effect, just one item, not a whole list, can come after a colon.

I forgot to pack the most important thing for the picnic: bug spray!

Don't use a colon after any words that are part of the verb *to be* (am, are, is, was, were, be, being, been).

The names of the deserts of Africa are Arabian, Kalahari, Libyan, Namib, Nubian, and Sahara.

USE A COLON AFTER HEADINGS IN A MEMO AND AFTER THE GREETING OF A BUSINESS LETTER

To: Mrs. Penn

From: Mrs. Freedman

Date: April 28, 2002

Subject: Our wonderful brother

Dear Chairman of the Board:

USE A COLON TO SEPARATE THE VOLUME NUMBER FROM THE PAGE NUMBER OF A BOOK, MAGAZINE, OR NEWSPAPER

The Encyclopedia of Animals X: 814 (volume X, page 814)

USE A COLON TO SEPARATE THE NUMBER OF THE CHAPTER FROM THE NUMBER OF THE VERSE OF THE BOOKS OF THE BIBLE

Luke 2:7 (chapter two, verse seven)

USE A COLON TO SEPARATE HOURS FROM MINUTES

3:25 p.m.   6:20 a.m.

USE A COLON TO SEPARATE THE PARTS OF A RATIO

On a scale of 60:1

USE A COLON TO SEPARATE A HEADING FROM WHAT FOLLOWS

DANGER: MAN-, WOMAN-, AND CHILD-EATING ALLIGATORS IN THIS RIVER!

USE A COLON TO SEPARATE THE TITLE OF A BOOK FROM ITS SUBTITLE

Pigs in My Kitchen: Life on a Farm

Some writers use a colon in a script of a play to separate the name of the character from what he or she says.

Roslyn: Keep those pigs out of my kitchen!

COMMAS

JOIN TWO INDEPENDENT CLAUSES WITH A COMMA AND A CONJUNCTION

Shana is in her last year of college, and her sister Sasha will soon graduate from high school.

See *Compound Sentence* on page 35.

PUT COMMAS BETWEEN THREE OR MORE INDEPENDENT CLAUSES IF THEY DON'T ALREADY HAVE COMMAS IN THEM

David does digital art on his computer, Jennifer designs original jewelry, and Karen is a special education teacher.

See *Independent Clause* on page 34.

PUT A COMMA AFTER A DEPENDENT CLAUSE THAT COMES BEFORE AN INDEPENDENT CLAUSE IN A COMPLEX SENTENCE

Because this is the first sunny day after two weeks of rain, I'm getting out of this house.

See *Clauses* on page 34 and *Complex Sentence* on page 35.

COLONS

PUT A COMMA BETWEEN ADJECTIVES THAT DESCRIBE THE SAME NOUN

He wore an amazing, astounding, fantastic costume to the Halloween party and won first prize.

See *Adjectives* on page 22.

PUT A COMMA AFTER A PREPOSITIONAL PHRASE THAT DOES THE JOB OF AN ADVERB

Underneath the rotting floor boards in the creaky cabin, Mistress Margo found Captain Bill's secret treasure chest.

See *Prepositional Phrases* on page 25 and *Adverbs* on page 23.

If the prepositional phrase is very short, you can skip the comma.

After today Max would be the Duke of North Conway.

PUT COMMAS AROUND PHRASES AND CLAUSES THAT GIVE INFORMATION BUT ARE NOT REALLY NECESSARY TO GET THE MAIN MEANING OF THE SENTENCE ACROSS

These phrases and clauses are called "nonrestrictive." They could be deleted from the sentence without really changing the main meaning of the sentence.

In 1828 the city of Philadelphia, which is in Pennsylvania, tried to sell the Liberty Bell for scrap metal.

FOR SALE CHEAP!

PUT A COMMA AFTER *YES, NO, OH,* AND SIMILAR MILD INTERJECTIONS AT THE BEGINNINGS OF SENTENCES

Oh, you want to marry me?

Yes, I'll do it.

No, I won't wear a pickle costume to the wedding.

Put an exclamation point after an interjection that shows strong feelings. See *Interjections* on page 28.

PUT A COMMA AFTER THE GREETING OF A PERSONAL LETTER AND AFTER THE CLOSE OF A PERSONAL OR BUSINESS LETTER

My dear Mrs. Scotto,   Hello, Glenn and Laurie,   Dear George,

Yours truly,   Sincerely,   Love,

USE A COMMA TO MAKE THE READER PAUSE SLIGHTLY TO AVOID POSSIBLE CONFUSION IN UNDERSTANDING THE MEANING OF A SENTENCE

Immediately before the flying fish flew away.

Immediately before, the flying fish flew away.

USE A COMMA TO SEPARATE TWO WORDS THAT ARE THE SAME IN A SENTENCE

When he spoke up up went my blood pressure.

When he spoke up, up went my blood pressure.

When business went down down went the stock.

When business went down, down went the stock.

USE COMMAS TO SEPARATE THREE OR MORE ITEMS IN A SERIES

Ellen, Fran, Peter, Bonnie, Sandra, Barbara, Miriam, Norma, and Harry are all members of my "Make the World Better" group.

USE A COMMA IN FRONT OF A DIRECT QUOTATION THAT DOES NOT BEGIN A SENTENCE

Ms. Markovits announced, "The trip to Boston has been postponed because the bus broke down."

See *Quotation Marks* on page 90.

USE A COMMA AT THE END OF THE FIRST PART OF A DIRECT QUOTATION THAT IS BROKEN UP IN A SENTENCE

"Come to my house for lunch," Loraine told Rozzie, "but please leave your gorilla at home because it scares my goldfish."

USE A COMMA BEFORE THE SECOND PART OF A DIRECT QUOTATION THAT IS BROKEN UP IN A SENTENCE

"I can't leave my gorilla at home alone," said Rozzie to Loraine, "because he's afraid to be by himself."

PUT A COMMA AFTER THE LAST WORD OF A DIRECT QUOTATION THAT IS A DECLARATIVE SENTENCE UNLESS THE LAST WORD OF THE DIRECT QUOTATION IS THE LAST WORD OF THE WHOLE SENTENCE

"Well, maybe your gorilla and my goldfish can be friends," said Loraine to Rozzie.

COMMAS

If the last word of a direct quotation is the last word of the whole sentence, put the appropriate punctuation mark after it (period, question mark, or exclamation point) followed by quotation marks.

>   Said Loraine to Rozzie, "Well, maybe your gorilla and my goldfish can be friends."

See *Declarative Sentence* on page 29.

PUT A COMMA AFTER A NOUN OF DIRECT ADDRESS THAT BEGINS A SENTENCE

>   Bonnie, will you please tell Kurt that his parakeet got an e-mail.

See *Noun of Direct Address* on page 19.

PUT A COMMA BEFORE A NOUN OF DIRECT ADDRESS THAT ENDS A SENTENCE

>   Please tell Kurt that his parakeet got an e-mail, Bonnie.

PUT COMMAS AROUND A NOUN OF DIRECT ADDRESS THAT IS IN THE MIDDLE OF A SENTENCE

>   Kurt's parakeet got an e-mail, Bonnie, so please ask the bird to put on its glasses and come to the computer.

USE ONE OR TWO COMMAS TO SET OFF APPOSITIVES AND OFFICIAL TITLES

>   William Jefferson Clinton, the forty-second president of the United States, was known as just "Bill," and James Earl Carter, the thirty-ninth president, was known as just "Jimmy."

See *Appositive* on page 21.

USE COMMAS TO SET OFF LITTLE EXPRESSIONS THAT BREAK THE FLOW OF THOUGHT IN A SENTENCE

>   Mrs. Potter, after all, was the dean, so all the kids had to do exactly what she said. Right?

USE A COMMA BEFORE AND AFTER ABBREVIATIONS LIKE *E.G.* AND *I.E.* AND WORDS LIKE *NAMELY*

He was suspended from school for many reasons, e.g., gluing the bathroom doors shut and letting the gerbils loose.

His behavior was considered atrocious, i.e., extremely cruel.

> e.g. is the Latin abbreviation for "for example."
>
> i.e. is the Latin abbreviation for "that is to say."

USE COMMAS TO SEPARATE PARTS OF AN ADDRESS IN A SENTENCE

They lived at 882 Fifty-first Street, Brooklyn, New York, until they sold the house and moved to 77 Shawmut Street, Chelsea, Massachusetts, in the 1940s.

USE COMMAS TO SEPARATE PARTS OF A DATE IN THE MIDDLE OF A SENTENCE (INCLUDING AFTER THE YEAR)

The two best dates in their lives were February 14, 1972, and July 19, 1976, because those are the days when their children were born.

If the date has only two parts to it, skip the comma.

Their children were born in February 1972 and July 1976.

USE A COMMA BEFORE AND AFTER *ETC.* IN THE MIDDLE OF A SENTENCE

Since *etc.* is an abbreviation for a Latin phrase that means "and so forth," it always has a period after it.

Lisa and Victor love to travel, cook, spend time with their children, juggle flaming torches, etc., but they have to be careful not to set the house on fire when they juggle the torches.

If *etc.* is the last word in the sentence, don't put a comma after it.

Jitka and Frank have been to Morocco, France, Italy, etc.

DASHES

When you interrupt your words with a definition, an example, a new fact, or a personal comment, and then go on, put a dash before and a dash after the interruption.

Last Thursday—a marvelous and terrible day—I won the trophy and then broke it.

The shortest girls on the basketball team—Karen, Marcy, Helene, Harriet, and Barbara—always score the most number of points.

See *Hyphens* on page 87.

USE A DASH AFTER A STATEMENT THAT IS INTERRUPTED OR UNFINISHED

The principal declared, "The winner of the Student-of-the-Year Award is—" but then the microphone suddenly went dead, so I didn't know if I had won.

USE A DASH BEFORE THE NAME OF A PERSON WHOSE WORDS YOU ARE QUOTING

The time is always ripe for doing right.

—Martin Luther King, Jr.

USE A DASH INSTEAD OF A COMMA BEFORE AN APPOSITIVE TO MAKE IT MORE DRAMATIC

It was only later that I realized that I had dropped the bowl of soup in the lap of Mr. Tim Williams—my new boss!

See *Appositive* on page 21.

> On a keyboard, a dash is two hyphens.

ELLIPSES

Three dots in a row is called an ellipsis. Use an ellipsis to show where you left words out of a quotation.

Original sentence (total–thirty-one words):

> Most people think that America's total and complete independence from Great Britain, the mother country across the great Atlantic Ocean, was formally and officially declared on the fourth of July, 1776.

> "Ellipsis" is singular.
> "Ellipses" is plural.

Shortened sentence with ellipses replacing the words that were cut out (total–seventeen words):

> Most people think that America's ... independence from Great Britain ... was ... declared on the fourth of July, 1776.

USE A PERIOD PLUS AN ELLIPSIS (ONE DOT PLUS THREE DOTS) TO SHOW THAT YOU LEFT WORDS OUT AT THE END OF A SENTENCE YOU ARE QUOTING

Original sentence:

> The members of the Continental Congress celebrated the event four days later on July 8, 1776, with a big parade, and most delegates didn't sign the Declaration of Independence until August 2, 1776.

Shortened sentence with words cut out at the end:

> The members of the Continental Congress celebrated the event four days later on July 8, 1776, with a big parade. ...

USE A PERIOD PLUS AN ELLIPSIS (ONE DOT PLUS THREE DOTS) TO SHOW THAT YOU LEFT OUT A WHOLE SENTENCE OR A WHOLE PARAGRAPH FROM A LONG QUOTATION

Original paragraph:

> Most people think that America's total and complete independence from Great Britain, the mother country across the great Atlantic Ocean, was formally and officially declared on the fourth of July, 1776. That is why today Independence Day is always celebrated with parades and fireworks on the Fourth of July. However, the truth is that the Continental Congress declared the "United Colonies Free and Independent States" on the second of July.

Shortened paragraph with one whole sentence deleted:

Most people think that America's total and complete independence from Great Britain, the mother country across the great Atlantic Ocean, was formally and officially declared on the fourth of July, 1776. . . . However, the truth is that the Continental Congress declared the "United Colonies Free and Independent States" on the second of July.

USE AN ELLIPSIS TO SHOW EXACTLY WHERE A PERSON HESITATED OR STOPPED SPEAKING FOR A MOMENT

When John asked Cindy to marry her, she said, "This is such a surprise to . . . I never knew you felt . . . I don't know what to . . . What did you say your name was?"

EXCLAMATION POINTS

Use an exclamation point at the end of an exclamatory sentence.

Three juggling seals are performing in the school yard right now**!**

See *Exclamatory Sentence* on page 30.

PUT AN EXCLAMATION POINT AT THE END OF AN IMPERATIVE SENTENCE THAT GIVES A STRONG ORDER OR COMMAND

Stop tickling me**!**

See *Imperative Sentence* on page 30.

Some people call exclamation points exclamation marks. Both terms are correct.

HYPHENS

A hyphen is like a dash, but it's shorter. A hyphen goes inside a word. A dash goes between words.

USE A HYPHEN IN SOME COMPOUND NOUNS AND IN COMPOUND ADJECTIVES THAT COME IN FRONT OF THE NOUNS THEY DESCRIBE

Most compound words are written as one word, but some are hyphenated.

close-up	all-time	custom-made	able-bodied
life-size	self-made	bad-tempered	above-ground

See *Compound Nouns* on page 17.

USE A HYPHEN TO MAKE A COMPOUND ADJECTIVE WITH THE PREFIX "WELL" WHEN THE ADJECTIVE IS USED IN FRONT OF THE NOUN IT DESCRIBES

well-fed	well-off	well-bred	well-done
well-knit	well-read	well-known	well-meant
well-worn	well-spoken	well-fixed	well-to-do

> The well-worn book was on the shelf.
>
> The book on the shelf was well worn.

USE A HYPHEN BETWEEN PREFIXES AND PROPER NOUNS AND ADJECTIVES

all-Italian specialties

mid-April carnival

pro-Western agreement

anti-American protests

non-Mexican cuisine

un-Elizabethan costumes

USE A HYPHEN TO SEPARATE A WORD INTO SYLLABLES WHEN THE WORD CAN'T FIT AT THE END OF A LINE

> "We have not failed," said Thomas Edison after so many ruined experiments." We now know a thou-sand things that won't work, so we are much clos-er to finding what will."

USE A HYPHEN WHEN YOU WRITE OUT NUMBERS FROM TWENTY-ONE TO NINETY-NINE IN WORDS

thirty-three   fifty-nine   sixty-four

You can write numbers as numbers starting with 100.

USE A HYPHEN IN FRACTIONS WRITTEN AS WORDS

three-eighths   one-third   four-fifths

USE A HYPHEN WHEN YOU SPELL WORDS OUT FOR DRAMATIC EFFECT

You are nuts. Nuts! N-u-t-s. Nuts!

USE A HYPHEN IN DOUBLE LAST NAMES

When Miss Tip married Mr. Top, they changed their name to Mr. and Mrs. Tip-Top.

USE A HYPHEN TO PREVENT CONFUSION BETWEEN WORDS

recollect: to remember   *recover*: to get back

re-collect: to collect again   *re-cover*: to cover again

As soon as I recover the use of my broken arm, I'll re-cover the sofa with new upholstery.

See *Prefixes* on page 52.

USE A HYPHEN AFTER SOME PREFIXES IF THE LAST LETTER OF THE PREFIX IS THE SAME AS THE FIRST LETTER OF THE BASE WORD

anti-inflation   pre-election

See *Prefixes* on page 52.

USE A HYPHEN TO MEAN "TO" OR "VS." BETWEEN YEARS, TIMES, NUMBERS, PAGES, PEOPLE, AND PLACES

On pages 21-28 in volume C-F, you will read about the famous Chicken-Turkey War (1742-1743) that was fought on the old Chelsea-Brooklyn road. Approximately 40-50 chickens mysteriously disappeared one dark, stormy night from 1-2 A.M. and were never seen again.

PARENTHESES

Put parentheses around extra words or an extra sentence that you put into your own writing (not something you are quoting) to give additional details, facts, opinions, or explanations.

> The newest computers (with over fifty gigabytes on the hard drives) are going on sale next Tuesday.

> The newest computers (I'd love to get one in purple stripes) are going on sale next Tuesday.

PUT PARENTHESES AROUND LETTERS OR NUMBERS IN A LIST

> To be punished, follow these directions exactly:
>
> **(1)** Take off your shoes and socks.
>
> **(2)** Wiggle your toes in the mud.
>
> **(3)** Go into your house.
>
> **(4)** Walk on the newly cleaned kitchen floor.

PUT PARENTHESES AROUND A QUESTION MARK TO SHOW THAT YOU'RE NOT 100 PERCENT SURE THAT A FACT IS ACCURATE

> The ballerina lost ninety-three **(?)** pounds on the seaweed and mashed potatoes diet.

Put parentheses around stage directions in the script of a play instead of brackets.

> Roslyn: **(**stomping her foot on the floor**)** Keep those pigs out of my kitchen!

PERIODS

PUT A PERIOD AT THE END OF A DECLARATIVE SENTENCE

Columbia Grammar and Prep School was founded in 1764.

See *Declarative Sentence* on page 29.

PUT A PERIOD AT THE END OF A MILD IMPERATIVE SENTENCE

Open your books to page 24 and answer questions 1, 2, and 6.

See *Imperative Sentence* on page 30.

PUT A PERIOD AFTER AN INITIAL IN A PERSON'S NAME

J. K. Rowling   Franklin D. Roosevelt   C. S. Lewis

PUT A PERIOD AFTER NUMBERS ON A LIST WHEN THE ITEMS ARE PRINTED ONE ON TOP OF THE OTHER

What to do on a Saturday morning:

1. Wake up
2. Get out of bed
3. Go to the bathroom
4. Get back into bed
5. Go back to sleep

PUT A PERIOD AFTER SOME ABBREVIATIONS

A.D.	B.C.	a.m.	B.A.	St.
Ave.	Rd.	Blvd.	M.D.	P.O.

Some abbreviations don't have periods. When in doubt, chec[k] your dictionary.

QUESTION MARKS

PUT A QUESTION MARK AT THE END OF A SENTENCE THAT ASKS A QUESTION

Is this the famous statue of King Cedric, the Chicken-Hearted, and his favorite pet, Magda the Mouse?

See *Interrogative Sentence* on page 30.

PUT A QUESTION MARK INSIDE A PAIR OF PARENTHESES AFTER A FACT, DATE, OR SPELLING THAT YOU'RE NOT SURE OF

In 2013 (?) a thousand space pioneers will blast off from Nevada (?) to colonize the planet Zizzle.

A question mark is not needed after an imperative sentence that sounds like a question but is really a polite request.

Would you kindly open that door and see if the monster is still in the closet.

QUOTATION MARKS

PUT QUOTATION MARKS AROUND WORDS YOU ARE QUOTING DIRECTLY IN A SENTENCE

"I am so happy that you are my very first class," announced the new teacher to the smiling students.

PUT QUOTATION MARKS AROUND WORDS THAT ARE MEANT TO BE SARCASTIC, MOCKING, IRONIC, OR SURPRISING, AND WORDS THAT GIVE DEFINITIONS OR EXPLANATIONS

I didn't know that "repugnant" meant "repulsive" when I called your brother that.

You leaned against the wet paint in your tuxedo? No wonder they call you "genius."

PUT QUOTATION MARKS AROUND THE TITLES OF

Chapters in a book: "The Scary Toenail"

Magazine or newspaper articles: "How to Boil a Turnip"

Songs: "Kiss My Tulips with Your Two Lips"

Episodes in a TV show: "Jessica's Modeling Job"

Speeches: "What I Learned in High School"

Poems: "Still, Still, Oh Beating of My Heart"

SEMICOLONS

USE A SEMICOLON TO JOIN TWO INDEPENDENT CLAUSES IN A COMPOUND SENTENCE

Justin's birthday is on Feb. 3; Amanda's is on Dec. 28.

See *Clauses* on page 34. See *Compound Sentence* on page 35.

USE A SEMICOLON WITH CERTAIN CONJUNCTIONS OR PHRASES IN COMPOUND SENTENCES

accordingly	also	as a result	on the other hand
besides	consequently	for example	
for instance	for this reason	furthermore	
hence	however	in addition	
in fact	indeed	moreover	
nevertheless	on the contrary	thus	
yet	that is	therefore	

> Remember: Independent Clause + Independent Clause = Compound Sentence

He lost his book-bag twenty-four times; therefore, his mother glued it to his jacket.

USE A SEMICOLON BETWEEN PHRASES OR CLAUSES IN A SERIES THAT ALREADY HAVE COMMAS IN THEM

At the supermarket I bought bananas, apples, and corn at the produce counter; chicken, hamburger, and bologna at the meat counter; cupcakes, bread, and cookies in the bakery; and paper plates, cups, and napkins in the paper goods section.

SLASHES

PUT A SPACE-SLASH-SPACE BETWEEN LINES IN A POEM WHEN YOU QUOTE A FEW IN A PARAGRAPH

She turned, brushed her hair from her face, and shouted to her dog: "A man who came from Zanzibar / Was playing songs on his guitar / I thought it seemed a bit bizarre / That he would claim he was the czar!" What could the dog say after that?

PUT A SLASH BETWEEN WORDS THAT YOU USE IN PAIRS

neither / nor   yes / no   hot / cold   up / down

PUT SLASHES BETWEEN PARTS OF AN INTERNET ADDRESS

http://www.thesaurus.com/Roget-Alpha-Index.html

Slashes in Internet addresses are sometimes called "forward slashes." Notice that colons, dots, and dashes are also used in Internet addresses.

UNDERLINES

PUT AN UNDERLINE UNDER THE TITLE OF A

Book: <u>Harry Potter and the Goblet of Fire</u>

Play, opera, or musical show: <u>You're a Good Man, Charlie Brown</u>

Magazine or newspaper: <u>Seventeen</u>, <u>Herald-Tribune</u>

Movie: <u>The Nutty Professor</u>

Radio or television program: <u>Animal Kingdom</u>

You can also put these titles into italics (*letters that slant to the right like this*) without underlines or into **boldface** if you want to.

Chapter 6
Getting Your Message Across

COMMUNICATING IDEAS

It's great to know about the parts of speech, spelling, punctuation, sentences, and paragraphs. But there's a lot more to communicating what you want to say to your readers in a way that will be interesting, understandable, and lively. You need to know a lot of vocabulary words, words that have the same and opposite meanings, words that can be really tricky, language that is imaginative and poetic, and special expressions and sayings.

VOCABULARY

Some word experts estimate that there are over 600,000 words in English, and more are being added all the time. In Shakespeare's day, about 400 years ago, there were only 50,000 words. The language has grown at least twelve times bigger since then!

But don't feel bad if you don't know what all those words mean. Nobody does, not even the people who write dictionaries. (They always have their own dictionaries nearby to look up words.) The person who knows the most English words (whoever he or she is) probably knows only a small fraction of the total number.

ENTIRE ENGLISH DICTIONARY ALL WORDS INCLUDED

But if you want to be a good writer and get all your ideas across most effectively, you need to build up your vocabulary.

Active and Passive Vocabularies

Everybody has an active vocabulary and a passive vocabulary.

Your active vocabulary contains all the words you use every day when you talk to your parents and friends and when you write letters and e-mails to people.

Your passive vocabulary is much bigger. It contains all the words that you understand if someone else uses them, but that you don't use regularly yourself.

There's also a kind of middle vocabulary, part active and part passive. It contains the words you use when speaking to teachers or other adults and the words you use when writing homework assignments like book reports and research papers.

Learning Vocabulary from Context

Readers can sometimes figure out what a word means, more or less, from its context (the words and sentences around the unknown word).

For instance, suppose you read:

> "His actions were considered heinous by everyone who knew about them."

You might not know what "heinous" means. Were his actions good or bad, smart or stupid, funny or serious? But if you read the sentence before or the sentence after, you might be able to make a reasonable guess about the meaning of "heinous."

> He had been in big trouble before, but now he surprised even those who already thought of him as a terrible person. His actions were considered heinous by everyone who knew about them. They were furious about what he had done. They could not forgive him. He would have to be punished.

If you guessed, after reading the whole paragraph, that "heinous" means "very bad, wicked, or terrible," you'd be absolutely right. If you carefully read the context of an unfamiliar word, all the words and sentences that surround that word, you can often arrive at a fairly good definition that fits that context.

Use Your Dictionary

Of course, if the context doesn't help, there's always the dictionary.

A good dictionary (in book form, a program on your computer, or downloaded from the Internet) is absolutely essential for any writer.

In addition to the definitions of a word, a good dictionary will tell you how to spell the word, how to pronounce it, what its part of speech is, what other forms the word has, its synonyms and antonyms, where it came from, what expressions it may appear in, and any special information you may need to know about it so that you don't confuse it with other words. That's a lot of important information for a writer.

Let's see how much you can learn from a dictionary about the meaning of a word you already know, "strike."

strike, v.

1. to hit or attack with the hand or an object
   She used to strike her big brother on the head with a feather duster.

2. to crash into
   The hot air balloon will strike the tree as it flies over.

3. to light on fire by scratching
   He always tries to strike a match to light the campfire.

4. to indicate time by a sound like a bong or ring
   All the church clocks in town strike the hour at the same time.

5. to have an effect or make an impression on someone
   It might strike the teacher as a good idea not to give homework today.

6. to find, come upon, or discover suddenly
   Did they strike gold in California in 1849 or 1850?

7. to refuse to work in order to get higher pay or better working conditions
   The women in the factory voted to strike if they didn't get raises.

Were you surprised to find seven different definitions of "strike," and those were only the verbs? These definitions can be found in a typical school dictionary. One college-level dictionary lists over thirty definitions of the verb "strike."

There are several other meanings for "strike" when it's used as a noun. *The pitcher threw three strikes and the batter was out. The bowler threw a strike with her very first ball. The air strike destroyed the village. The telephone workers' strike lasted two weeks.*

A good dictionary will also tell you that "struck" is the past tense of the verb, and that the word is used in expressions like "strike out," strike up the band," "strike it rich," "strike a happy medium," and "strike while the iron is hot."

A good dictionary can give a writer like you a ton of valuable, fascinating information.

How to Build up Your Vocabulary

- Don't let a strange word escape you. When you come upon a new word, circle it, underline it, highlight it—do something to make it stand out. If you can't write on the page, use stick-on notes.

- Try to figure out the meaning of the word from its context.

- Look the word up in the closest dictionary (in a book or on your computer).

- Write the definition down in a handy notebook of new words or on blank flashcards. Later, look over your new words and their definitions. Think about them. Try to learn them.

- Use the new words as soon as you can in conversation or in a school paper. The more you use a word, the better you know it.

Building up your vocabulary is a lifelong activity. You might be surprised to know that adults look words up all the time, even your English teacher!

See *Learning Vocabulary from Context* on page 94.

You'll never know the meanings of all the words in English (nobody has, does, or ever will know them all), but your vocabulary will grow and grow.

There are many words in English that you have to be especially careful about because they're so tricky. And there are lots of words that have the same or opposite meanings. You'll find out about them in the sections on *Homonyms, Homographs,* and *Synonyms and Antonyms* later in this chapter.

HOMONYMS/HOMOPHONES

Some people call homonyms homophones. Whatever you or your teacher calls them, here's what they are.

Homonyms are words that are pronounced exactly like other words but have different spellings and different meanings.

Homonyms can play nasty tricks on your spell checker, so it's important to be able to tell them apart and use them correctly.

See *What About Spell Checkers?* on page 39.

Here are some of the homonyms that befuddle writers the most. If you're not sure of what some of them mean, check your dictionary.

We are not **allowed** to talk **aloud** in the library.

The construction crew will **alter** the church **altar**.

Last night I **ate** about **eight** of those frosted donuts.

He plays **bass** fiddle in the band and third **base** on the team.

She started to **bawl** when she got hit by the **ball**.

When will that **bee** ever **be** back at this flower?

Little Boy **Blue** said he **blew** his horn.

The **bow** of the ship is made from the **bough** of a tree.

Don't hit the **brake** of your bike too hard or you'll **break** it.

When you walk **by** the store, **buy** some milk. **'Bye** for now.

The state **capitol** building is in the **capital** city of the state.

In each box of the **cereal** was another chapter in the **serial**.

He may **choose** the kind of gum he **chews**.

I'm asking the student **council** to **counsel** me in this matter.

Take a language **course** to improve your **coarse** language.

This gold **cymbal** is a **symbol** of the success of our band.

The baby **deer** in the petting zoo was such a **dear** thing.

It takes **dual** weapons to fight a **duel**.

Does a pottery worker **earn** a lot for making an **urn**?

Flee, oh tiny **flea**, before you get squished.

Down the windy **flue** of the chimney **flew** the sickening **flu**.

The farmer raised a clean chicken, not a **foul** that was **fowl**.

The **fourth** marching band in the parade marched **forth**.

The animal covered in **fur** stood under the **fir** tree.

The **gnu** really **knew** the old zoo, not the **new** zoo.

Rabbit fur is sometimes called "**hair** of the **hare**."

The pilot's coat hangs on a **hanger** in the airplane **hangar**.

The cowboy **heard** a thundering **herd** of cattle passing by.

The **heir** to the throne breathed in some fresh **air**.

A foot doctor's job: **he'll** try to **heal** your sore **heel**.

Put your ear **here** and you'll **hear** the mysterious sound.

Hie (hurry) up the **high** hill to say **hi** to the climbers.

This sore throat spray is for my **horse** who is **hoarse**.

This quiet **hour** is **our** special time together.

At my island wedding, **I'll** walk down the **aisle** on the **isle**.

The miner **led** me to the **lead** ore in the cave.

To **lessen** the difficulty of the **lesson**, add humor to it.

This is the **lone** bank that will **loan** me money.

The new **maid** has **made** the beds very nicely.

In **Maine** you'll see an animal with a **mane** in the **main** zoo.

That little insect **might** be a **mite** or a tick.

At **night**, the **knight** takes off his shining armor for the day.

No, I do not **know** the answer to every question.

I am **not** very good at tying this complicated **knot**.

Use this **oar** to row to the cave, **or** you won't find the **ore**.

She lifted the heavy **pail**, turned **pale**, and fainted.

A doctor must have **patience** to deal with her **patients**.

When I heard the bell **peal**, I slipped on the banana **peel**.

If they give up this **piece** of land, there will be **peace**.

He works on the **pier** and feels he is everyone's **peer**.

Pray for the animals that other animals **prey** on.

The **principal** instills the **principle** of honesty in students.

Rain fell on the horse's **rein** in the king's **reign**.

I **read** the blue book, the green book, and the **red** book.

Read the directions on how to fit the **reed** on your clarinet.

She will **write** out the **right** words to the ceremonial **rite**.

On my **route** through the woods, I tripped on a tree **root**.

I'll **sail** across the lake to get bargains at the big **sale**.

The **scent** she **sent** me to buy cost more than a **cent**.

From the top of the lighthouse you can **see** miles of **sea**.

The warden of the prison would not **sell** me a jail **cell**.

Sew up the seed bag **so** you can **sow** the seeds.

The lovely **site** on the postcard was a **sight** for sore eyes.

She rode her **sleigh** into the giant's woods to **slay** him.

The poor bird couldn't **soar** because its wings were **sore**.

Some people think that this **sum** is too high.

Cover your **son** with **sun** block so he won't get a burn.

Walking is good for the **soul**, but the **sole** of my foot hurts.

I'll pound a **stake** into the ground, and you cook us a **steak**.

The **stationery** store doesn't move, so it's **stationary**.

The police arrested them for trying to **steal** the **steel**.

The captain sailed **straight** through the dangerous **strait**.

He wove a fascinating **tale** about the **tail** of the golden lion.

The stadium will **teem** with people to see our **team** play.

They're telling me that **their** car is parked over **there**.

Two people are **too** many **to** sit on one seat.

The weather **vane** fell and cut the **vein** of the **vain** man.

If you stop eating so much, your thick **waist** will **waste** away.

Wait a minute, and I'll tell you the **weight** of your package.

The **weather** will determine **whether** we stay in or go out.

He got sick, and for a **week** he felt very **weak**.

Where do you have to **wear** a tuxedo in a hard**ware** store?

Which broomstick belongs to the **witch**?

He dug a **whole** ton of dirt out of the **hole**.

Who's claiming **whose** kid is smarter?

On the television quiz show, he **won** only **one** dollar.

Thanks for saying that **you're** sorry for **your** mistake.

HOMOGRAPHS

Homographs are words that are spelled exactly alike but have different sounds and different meanings.

Homographs are the opposite of homonyms.

Homonyms:	different spellings	same sound
Homographs:	same spelling	different sounds

Some books say that homographs can be words that have the same sound but different meanings and origins, but the trickiest homographs are the ones with different sounds. Those are the ones we'll learn about in this chapter.

The words in parentheses are words that rhyme with or sound like the homographs. They will help you pronounce the homographs correctly. Definitions of the words are in italics *(letters that slant to the right).*

bass (rhymes with face): *a low-pitched sound*
bass (rhymes with pass): *a type of fish*
The **bass** singer loves to fish for **bass**.

bow (rhymes with no): *a knot with two loops*
bow (rhymes with now): *to bend downward from the waist*
Put this **bow** on your head and take a **bow**.

desert (sounds like duh-**zert**): *to abandon, withdraw from*
desert (sounds like **dez**-ert): *a dry, barren, sandy place*
Never **desert** your post on the hot **desert**.

do (rhymes with goo): *to carry out a task*
do (rhymes with go): *the first note on the scale*
Please **do** sing the scale starting with the note **do**.

does (rhymes with fuzz): *present tense of the verb "to do"*
does (rhymes with foes): female deer
Does this zoo have any **does**?

dove (rhymes with love): *a bird associated with peace*
dove (rhymes with stove): *past tense of "to dive"*
A beautiful **dove dove** out of the sky and swooped down.

drawer (rhymes with saw): *boxlike compartment in a piece of furniture that can be pulled out*
drawer (sounds like draw-er): *a person who draws*
Into the dresser **drawer**, the **drawer** put her drawings.

lead (rhymes with seed): *to show the way*
lead (rhymes with said): *a soft, dense metal*
Will you **lead** me right to the stockpile of **lead**?

Lima (sounds like "**lee**-muh"): *capital city of Peru*
lima (rhymes with "I'm a"): *a large, light green bean*
In **Lima** they love to eat **lima** beans for dinner.

live (rhymes with give): *to be alive*
live (rhymes with drive): *having life*
I want to **live** long enough to meet a **live** alien from space.

minute (rhymes with "in it"): *sixty seconds*
minute (rhymes with "my boot"): *exceptionally tiny*
In a **minute** we'll see **minute** atomic particles on the screen.

Polish (pronounced **poh**-lish): *of or relating to Poland*
polish (pronounced **paw**-lish): *liquid used to shine a surface*
The **Polish** company developed a new furniture **polish**.

read (sounds like reed): *to understand printed words*
read (sounds like red): *past tense of "to read"*
Read this book and you'll have **read** every book in the library.

row (rhymes with no): *a series of objects in a straight line*
row (rhymes with now): *a big quarrel*
He knocked over her **row** of blocks, and they had a big **row**.

sow (rhymes with no): *to scatter seeds for growing*
sow (rhymes with now): *an adult female hog*
If you **sow** the seeds today, that big **sow** might eat them.

tear (rhymes with chair): *to rip apart*

tear (rhymes with cheer): *a drop of water from an eye*

When she saw him **tear** up her picture, a **tear** came to her eye.

wind (rhymes with find): *to wrap something around*

wind (rhymes with sinned): *air that is moving*

It's impossible to **wind** up the string of this kite in this **wind**.

wound (rhymes with found): *past tense of "to wind"*

wound (rhymes with crooned): *an injury*

The nurse **wound** the bandage tightly around his **wound**.

FIGURES OF SPEECH

Writers who want to be really creative and express themselves in imaginative ways often use Figures of Speech. These are special ways of using words and phrases to paint vivid, sharp word pictures for readers. People who write poetry use figures of speech a lot, but anyone writing anything can use them to add color and imagination to his or her words.

> Figures of Speech are not Parts of Speech, although you do use Parts of Speech (nouns, verbs, adjectives, etc.) to create Figures of Speech. See *Parts of Speech* on page 11.

Alliteration

Alliteration is when words close together begin with the same sound (not necessarily the same letter).

A perfect example of alliteration is the old tongue-twister:

Peter Piper picked a peck of pickled peppers.

"Alliteration" is pronounced *uh-lit-uh-**ray**-shun*

USE ALLITERATION IN YOUR WRITING TO

Create a mood:
The day dawned damp, dreary, and drab.

Add a bit of humor:
Felix Fluster fell flat on his fanny.

Give a character a unique name:
George G. Giraffe

Create drama:
The hazardous hurricane howls heart-lessly through the hollow hills.

Reproduce a sound:
Chattering cheerfully, the chipmunks chirped and chuckled.

Label something:
Katie's Christmas Candies

Note that the last example at left, *Katie's Christmas Candies*, is an example of alliteration because the three words all begin with the same sound even though the sounds are made with different letters: **K**, **Ch**, and **C**.

Hyperbole

Hyperboles are over-the-top exaggerations used for special effect.

"Hyperbole" is pronounced high-**per**-bow-lee.

Readers don't really believe 100% of what they're reading when they see a hyperbole. They know that hyperboles are used to add emphasis and create dramatic, amusing, or remarkable images.

For instance, suppose you read:

The captain of our basketball team is so tall that he wears a hat with a flashing red light so that helicopters won't bump into his head.

You would know that the writer made up the hat with the red light just to create an exaggerated image of a very tall person.

Use hyperboles in your writing to describe a scene or person in a dramatic, funny, or surprising way that will make the image striking and memorable.

Here are more examples of hyperbole.

We're having a heat wave. The sidewalks are bubbling, the buildings are sweating, and the trees are fanning themselves.

My grandmother could speak about a million languages.

My teacher was so skinny she came into the classroom through the keyhole in the door.

I have so much homework, I'll be about ninety-nine years old when I finish it.

Similes

Similes are creative comparisons using the words "like" or "as." They show imaginative relationships between objects and people that are not alike.

Sometimes, to make an image very vivid, a writer uses an unusual comparison so that the reader will get the picture more sharply.

"Simile" is pronounced **sim**-i-lee.

pretty as a picture

sweet as honey

quiet as a mouse

stubborn as a mule

slow as molasses

works like a horse

has cheeks like roses

stings like a bee

sings like a nightingale

waddles like a duck

Clichés:
Overused expressions, like some of those used as examples in this chapter, are called *clichés* (pronounced: *clee-***shays**). Once they were new and surprising, but with overuse they have become stale. Try to avoid clichés in your writing. If you've seen it many times before, don't use it yourself. Try to think of new ways of expressing your ideas.

Here are some very striking similes.

It's as ridiculous as looking for hot water under the sea.
—Old Latin proverb

Baseball games are like snowflakes and fingerprints. No two are ever alike.
—W. P. Kinsella

His hair stood upright like porcupine quills.
—Boccaccio

Happy as a butterfly in a garden full of sunshine and flowers.
—Louisa May Alcott

The mountains were jagged like a page ripped out of a book.
—Kate Grenville

[She] holds a . . . yellow tennis ball up in front of her like the torch on the Statue of Liberty.
—Daphne Merkin

A thunderstorm came rushing down . . . roaring like a brontosaur.
—Carlos Baker

Metaphors

A metaphor makes a comparison between unlike objects without using the words "like" or "as."

Similes:

My new mattress is as soft *as* a cloud.

My new mattress is *like* a soft cloud.

Metaphor:

I sleep on a soft cloud, my new mattress.

A simile tells you that something is *like* another thing.

A metaphor tells you that something *is* another thing.

"Metaphor" is pronounced **met**-uh-four.

Here are some metaphors.

She was a moving van, loaded down with all her kids' toys, food, books, clothing, and the kids, too!

I need a new hand cream because my skin is sandpaper.

A good book is a swift ship that sails you on exciting adventures.

He works overtime to pay the mountain of bills he faces.

My math teacher was a human calculator.

Onomatopoeia

Onomatopoeia is the use of words that imitate the sounds of sounds.

As you write, you want your readers to experience the full sensations of the scenes you are describing: the sights, smells, tastes, textures, and the sounds. Onomatopoeia is the figure of speech that helps you with the sound effects.

"Onomatopoeia" is pronounced *on-uh-mat-uh-**pee**-uh.*

See how onomatopoeia helps make the description of the scene below more powerful through the use of sound words.

The burning logs **crackled** in the fireplace as the clock **tick-tocked** its way into the night. Outside, the shutters **whacked** against the side of the house as the wind **howled**, the thunder **rumbled** in the distance, and the trees **creaked**. An old owl **hooted** behind the barn, while back inside the house, the **squeak** of a little mouse aroused the **purring** cat.

Here are some other onomatopoetic words you can use to make your writing sound more exciting.

clomp	roar	screech	hiss
smack	click	chirp	pop
bong	rustle	honk	clang
boom	slurp	squish	buzz
clatter	hum	squeal	peep
clack	ping	clink	splash
whiz	splash	thud	
bang	quack	thump	
crunch	ring	fizz	
cluck	sizzle	plop	

Personification

Personification means giving the qualities of people to things that are not alive.

A cloud is not a person. But if a writer writes that a "cloud cried tears," instead of "it rained," the writer is personifying the cloud, suggesting that the cloud can weep like a person.

> "Personification" is pronounced *per-sohn-i-fih-**kay**-shun.*

In the paragraph below, see how the use of personification seems to make the forces of nature come alive by giving them human qualities (the ability to punch, dance, wave, warn, duck, throw things, bark threats, pour water, etc.).

An unexpected gust of wind came around the corner and punched me in the nose. I dropped my newspaper, which did a swirling dance across the street. The trees waved their arms wildly, warning me to hurry home. The sun suddenly ducked behind the nearest cloud, and the sky threw bolts of lightning to the earth as loud thunder barked its threats at me. Next the heavens poured a tub of water on my head. My poor umbrella surrendered itself to the storm, blew out of my hands, and escaped into the darkness. I tried to do the same.

> Use personification in your writing to paint vivid word pictures in your readers' minds, pictures that show that things can look or act like people.

With personification, you can make a flower smile at a bee, a mountain guard a valley, a penguin wear a tuxedo, and a tea kettle whistle a tune.

IDIOMS

Idioms are special expressions and sayings.

These phrases were made up years, even centuries, ago. Experienced readers are usually familiar with most idioms and understand what they mean even though the individual words take on new meanings when used together.

For instance, if someone tells you to "mind your P's and Q's," she's asking you to be on your best behavior, to be careful to mind your manners. This expression is at least 400 years old, and word experts think it could have at least three possible origins:

1. the letters "p" and "q" can be confused, so you have to be extra careful about them

2. in old English pubs people had to pay for the "pints" and "quarts" they drank

3. "pieds" and "queues" are dance steps that French dancers had to perform carefully

Today it doesn't really matter how an idiom originated as long as you know what it means.

See *Clichés* on page 104.

There are thousands of idioms in the English language. Here is a sampling of some of the best known from A to Z.

Use an idiom in your writing when it perfectly fits what you're trying to express, but be careful not to overdo it. Most idioms are so familiar that they're clichés, and you want your writing to be fresh and original.

Ants in your pants
very restless, can't sit still

Barking up the wrong tree
having the wrong idea about something

Cat got your tongue?
Why don't you speak?

Don't count your chickens before they hatch.
Don't be too sure that things are going to work out the way you think they will until they do.

Every cloud has a silver lining.
In every bad situation there is something good.

Feather in your cap
an honor or accomplishment to be proud of

Get up on the wrong side of the bed
to wake up in a grumpy, grouchy mood

Hard nut to crack
a very difficult problem to solve

In hot water
in a lot of trouble

Jump down someone's throat
to scream or yell at someone angrily

Keep your shirt on.
stay calm; don't get angry; be patient

Lay an egg
to fail totally at something; give an embarrassing performance

Make a mountain out of a molehill
to make a small issue into an important one by exaggerating it

Needle in a haystack
something very hard to find

Out of the woods
safe from danger or trouble

Pen is mightier than the sword.
Writing about something accomplishes more than fighting about it.

Quick on the draw
mentally alert; quick to learn new things; fast to respond

Red tape
rules and regulations that waste a lot of time

Security blanket
something you hold onto that makes you feel safer

Tickled pink
very happy, amused, delighted, or pleased

Upset the apple cart
to spoil a plan suddenly or accidentally

Variety is the spice of life
new things make life more interesting

Wet behind the ears
inexperienced, new to the job, young

X marks the spot.
This is the exact location or place we want or are looking for.

You can't teach an old dog new tricks.
Some people are set in their ways and don't want to try new things.

Zip it up!
Be quiet. Stop talking.

SYNONYMS AND ANTONYMS

Synonyms Are Words That Have the Same Meaning

Because there are so many words in the English language, there are often many different words you can choose that will express your thoughts perfectly.

For instance, you could write that the monster was *big*. But to make your sentence more dramatic and emphatic, you could write that he was *huge, immense, gigantic, enormous, mammoth, tremendous, titanic, colossal, massive,* or *gargantuan*. Wow!

All those words are synonyms of "big." The "**s**" in "**s**ynonym" should remind you of "**s**ame meaning."

Antonyms Are Words with Opposite Meanings

The opposite of synonym is "antonym."

Suppose, in your story, a small person, the very opposite of the giant, was going to fight the big guy. You could describe this person as "small," of course, or you could use one of the many antonyms of "big" to emphasize how opposite your two characters are: *tiny, little, diminutive, miniature, minute, infinitesimal, minuscule, microscopic, teensy-weensy, itty-bitty,* and *Lilliputian*.

Where do you find all these synonyms and antonyms? In a special book called a "thesaurus." A thesaurus is a listing of thousands of words and their synonyms and antonyms. No writer should ever be without a good thesaurus. Many word processing programs have thesauruses built in. Learn how to use yours so you can add new, colorful, expressive words to your writing.

Here are some examples of synonyms and antonyms for just the common, everyday word "good" that you can find in a typical thesaurus.

"good"	
syn	*ant*
nice	decayed
acceptable	deficient
adequate	deleterious
advantageous	detrimental
all right	disagreeable
appropriate	displeasing
beneficial	dissatisfactory
brave	ill-behaved
convenient	improper
favorable	inadequate
favoring	inauspicious
fit	inferior
helpful	injurious
proper	misbehaving
propitious	poor
satisfactory	putrid
sufficient	rotten
suitable	spoiled
tolerable	unacceptable
useful	unfavorable
moral	unpleasant
upright	unsatisfactory
virtuous	wrong

In your thesaurus or dictionary, *syn* means synonyms and *ant* means antonyms.

DATE DUE

JUL 2 7 2009	
JAN 2 5 2010	
FEB 2 5 2010	